Kim and Mario Build

a Labyrinth and So Can You

Also By Kim Antieau

Novels

The Blue Tail • Broken Moon • Butch
Church of the Old Mermaids • Coyote Cowgirl
Deathmark • The Desert Siren • The Fish Wife
The Gaia Websters • Her Frozen Wild
Jewelweed Station • The Jigsaw Woman
Killing Beauty • Mercy, Unbound
The Monster's Daughter
Queendom: Feast of the Saints
Ruby's Imagine • Swans in Winter • The Rift
Whackadoodle Times • Whackadoodle Times Two

Nonfiction

Answering the Creative Call
Certified
Counting on Wildflowers
The Old Mermaids Book of Days and Nights
The Old Mermaids Book of Days and Nights: A Year
*   and a Day Journal*
An Old Mermaid Journal • The Salmon Mysteries
Under the Tucson Moon

Short Story Collections

Entangled Realities (with Mario Milosevic)
The First Book of Old Mermaids Tales
Tales Fabulous and Fairy
Trudging to Eden

Also By Mario Milosevic

Novels

Claypot Dreamstance
The Coma Monologues
The Doctor and the Clown
Kyle's War
The Last Giant
Splitting
Terrastina and Mazolli

Collections

Entangled Realities (with Kim Antieau)
Labor Days
Miniatures
Mostly Invisible
20 Strange Tales of Crime and Mystery

Poetry

Animal Life
Fantasy Life
Love Life

Kim and Mario Build a Labyrinth and So Can You

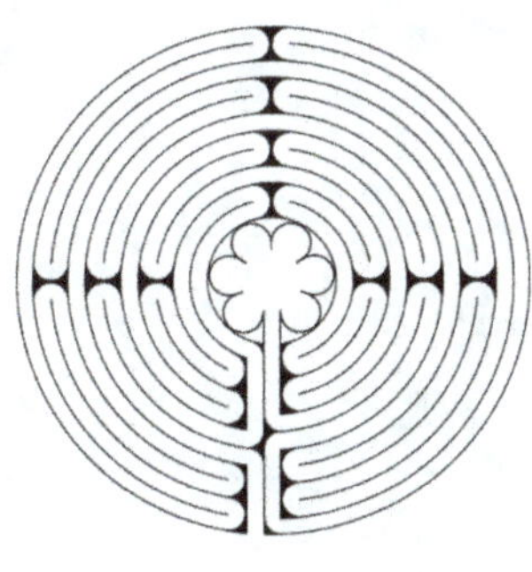

Kim Antieau and Mario Milosevic

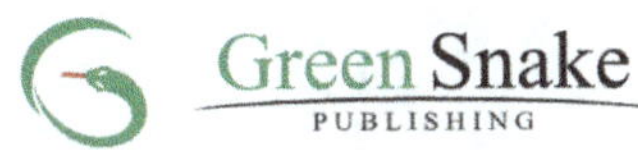

Green Snake
PUBLISHING

Kim and Mario Build a Labyrinth and So Can You
by Kim Antieau and Mario Milosevic

Copyright © 2020 by Kim Antieau and Mario Milosevic

ISBN: 978-1-949644-60-9

Photos by Kim Antieau.
Labyrinth diagrams by Mario Milosevic.

Thanks to Nancy Milosevic.

Published by Green Snake Publishing.
www.greensnakepublishing.com

Contents

Introduction: A Memoir and a How-To

This is the story of how we built our labyrinth. We had a lot of fun putting our labyrinth together and wanted to write a book about it to tell the world.

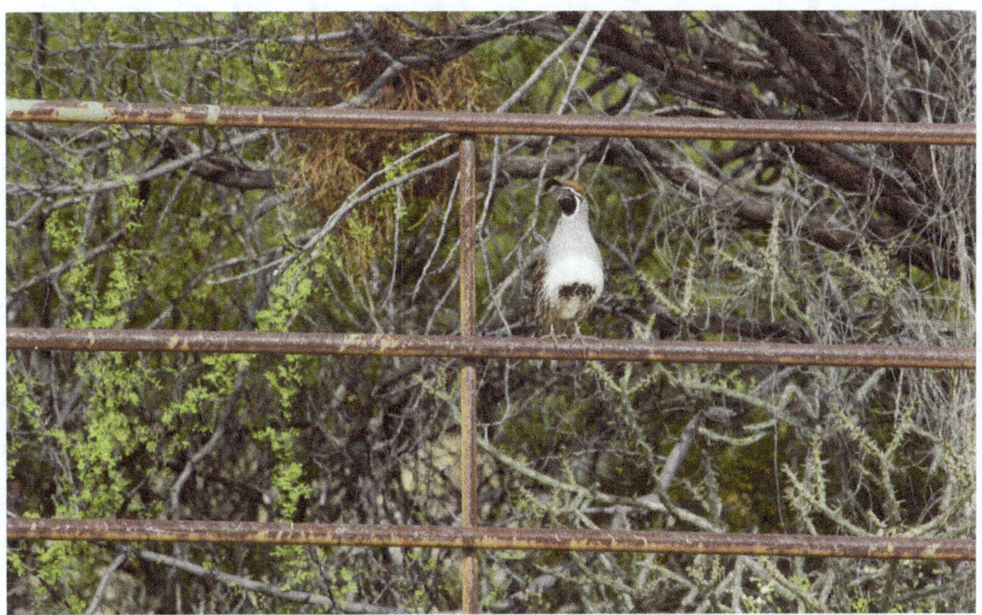

One of our feathered friends observing us while we build our labyrinth.

Walking a labyrinth is a wonderful experience. Building one just adds to the wonder.

We also intend this little book to be a guide for how you can build your own labyrinth.

We had some false starts and occasionally stumbled along the way. We have mostly left those stumbles out of our account so that someone who wants to use this book to build their own labyrinth can have a relatively clear path from beginning to end.

With all that in mind, come with us as we tell the story of the Old Mermaids Sanctuary Labyrinth.

Location, Location, Location

Where to put a labyrinth? It's up to you, of course, but you will most likely need to find a place with some elbow room. The original Chartres Labyrinth in France, the model for the one in this book, is 42 feet in diameter. Naturally, your labyrinth can be as small or as big as you want it to be. But for a good-sized labyrinth, one that feels expansive and that is a joy to walk, more space is generally better than less space.

Indoors or outdoors? An indoor setting can be serene and protected from the weather. You can find sites online that will guide you through making an indoor labyrinth on a floor using masking tape. We have walked many indoor labyrinths in gymnasiums and churches, but for us, they lack a certain magic. Where is nature? Where are the stars and the sky? Where is the breeze on your cheek?

Walking a labyrinth outdoors, under a full moon, say, or with the sun rising and splashing light on you and your path can add a special measure of enchantment all its own. Not to mention the sheer pleasure of feeling the ground beneath your feet as you take each step into and out of the center.

Treading on dirt, grass, or gravel just feels more connected to the spirit of what a labyrinth offers a walker. That's why this book describes how to build an outdoor labyrinth. More specifically, *our* outdoor labyrinth.

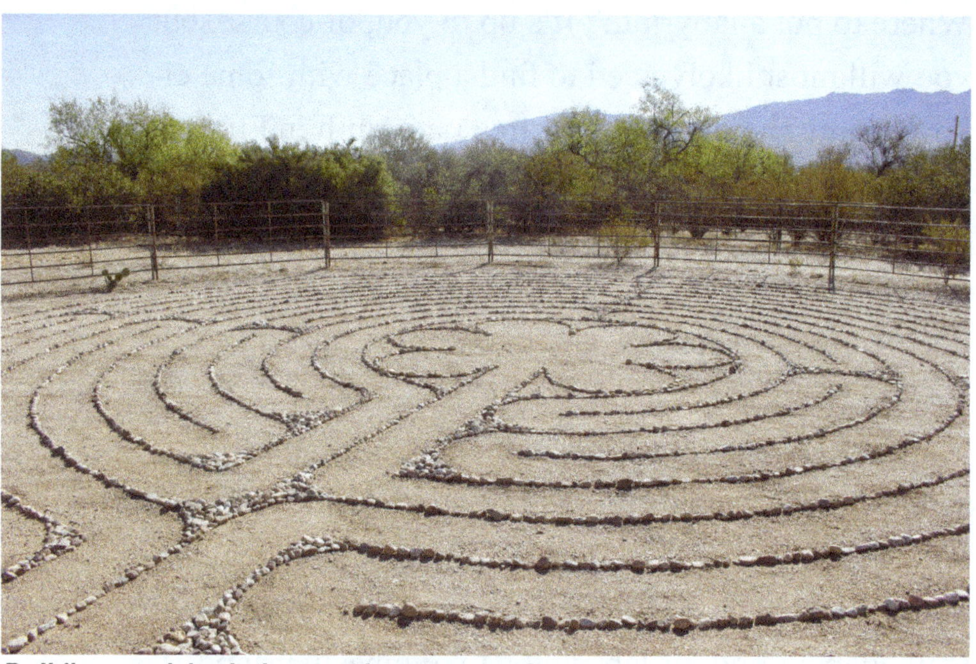

Building our labyrinth was a joyous experience.

So the first order of business is acquiring a plot of land or the use of some land.

For the labyrinth we're going to be talking about here, the acquisition of the land was a happy confluence of events that felt both surprising and inevitable.

We had been coming to a house in the Sonoran Desert just outside of Tucson for many winters. It was a retreat for artists and writers, and we cherished our time there. We thought of the little studio apartment we lived in for those weeks we were here as our second home. We did a lot of creative work here, writing novels, mostly, and reveling in the land and the wildlife that was abundant everywhere on and near the property.

We wrote many books here. One of them, *Church of the Old Mermaids*, by Kim, was inspired by the land, the wash, and the house here. We started calling the place the Old Mermaids Sanctuary—or the Sanctuary for short.

The house eventually sold to new owners, and our retreat was no more. We still came to Tucson regularly, but we missed our home away from home at the Sanctuary.

During our annual retreats we fell in love with the Sonoran Desert. When we were ready to move out of our rented house in Washington state, we came to Tucson to look for a modest house to buy.

Lo and behold, the property that we had visited all those past winters—the Old Mermaids Sanctuary— was unexpectedly for sale again. The new owners, after only five years, were selling the property. This was completely unexpected and felt like a sign from the Universe.

We discovered this happy circumstance one afternoon when, on a whim, we drove by the house and saw a FOR SALE sign at the end of the driveway. Even our real estate agent didn't know the house was on the market. It turned out that it was going up for sale the very next day and the owners had put the sign out a day early in preparation.

We begged to see the place before it officially went up for sale. The next day we went to the Sanctuary and knew immediately that we wanted to buy it. We tossed out the idea of a modest little house and threw our fates in with this enchanted sanctuary in the toes of the foothills of the Rincon Mountains with gorgeous views of the Catalina Mountains to the north and numerous daily visitors in the form of roadrunners, javelinas, rabbits, lizards, hummingbirds, owls, and more. It is a cherished refuge, and we were excited that we had a chance to own it.

We made an offer that afternoon. It was accepted before the close of business that day.

The next couple of months were a whirlwind of documents, inspections, seemingly endless check-writing, bewildering legal mumbo-jumbo, invasive inquiries from our mortgage company, and packing.

It was head-spinning and turned one of us (Mario)

into a nervous wreck. Could we afford this house?
Were we ready to be home owners? What if things
started breaking down on us? And, most importantly,
could we afford *this* house? The Old Mermaids Sanctuary was our first purchase of real estate, and we
were somewhat overwhelmed by all that house buying
entails.

But everything worked out, and we now own
(along with the bank) a house on 4.4 desert acres stud-
ded with saguaro, palo verde, mesquite, and prickly
pear, and home to a wide assortment of wildlife.

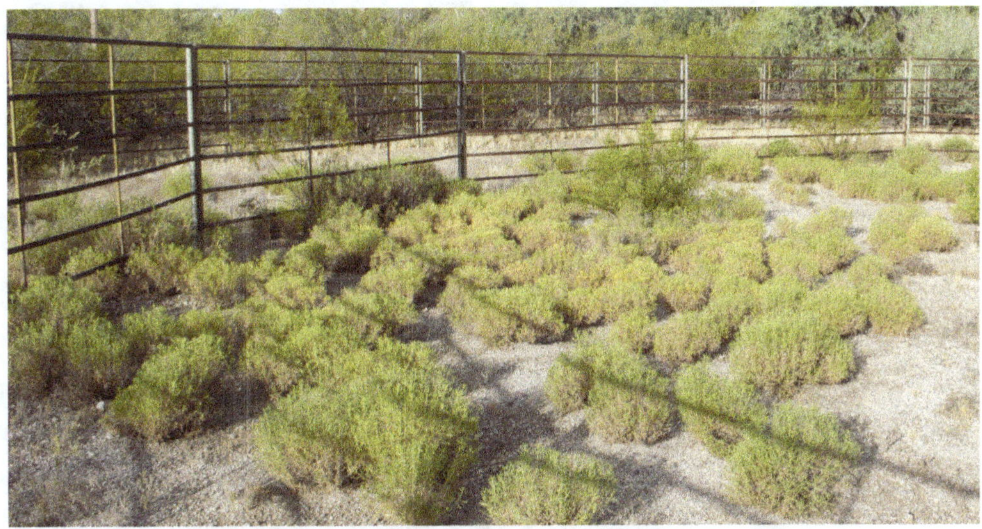

*The round corral within the oval corral, thick with desert
broom. The site of the future labyrinth.*

The land includes three horse corrals. We aren't in-
terested in keeping or boarding horses, but one of the
corrals, which is approximately 200 feet long, has a

second round corral inside it (a bull pen.) It is 60 feet in diameter.

We knew as soon as we saw this circular enclosure that it would be a perfect setting for a labyrinth, and we told each other we would construct one soon.

Clearing the Land

Easier said than done!

Even though the soil here is dry and crumbly and the weather can be brutally hot, many plants not only survive but thrive in the harsh conditions. Case in

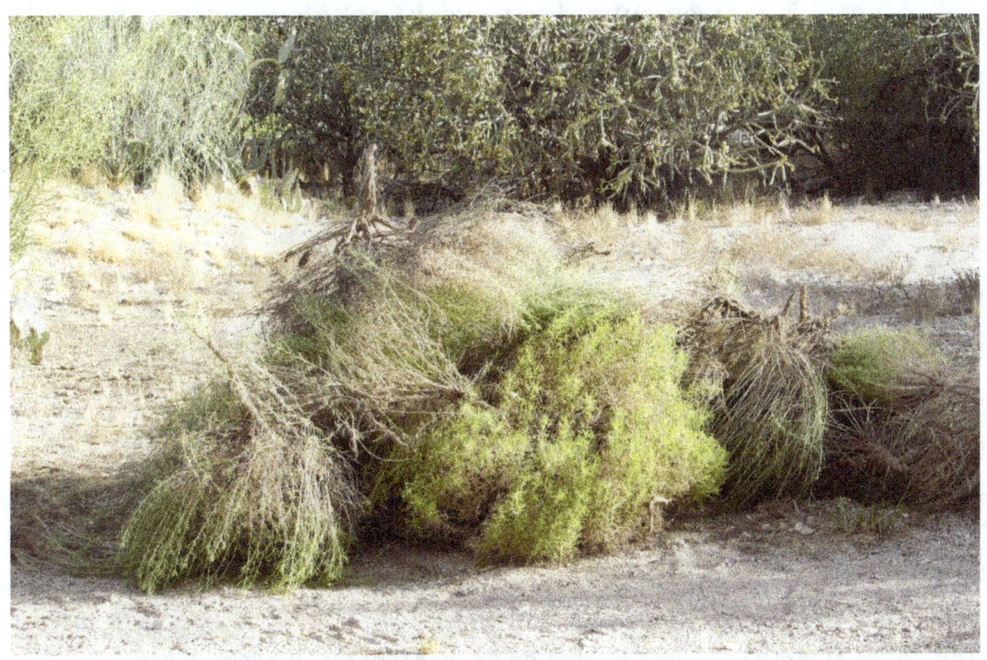

Pulled desert broom ready to be hauled away.

point: the circular corral was dense with over a dozen medium-sized mesquite trees and thick with hundreds of desert broom plants.

All those plants would have to be removed to make room for our labyrinth. It took about two weeks of early morning work (before it got too hot) to pull up all the mesquite and desert broom. We mostly used a pitchfork with thick tines. Our method was to wedge two tines around the woody stems of the plants, then pull up on the handle, using brute strength to leverage the roots right out of the ground. This worked for most of the plants. A few needed some extra excavation with a good old-fashioned shovel. And for some, the roots were too big to pull up, and we had to remove the plant and leave the roots.

It was sweaty, dusty work, but also methodical and meditative. In the end, when all was said and done, we

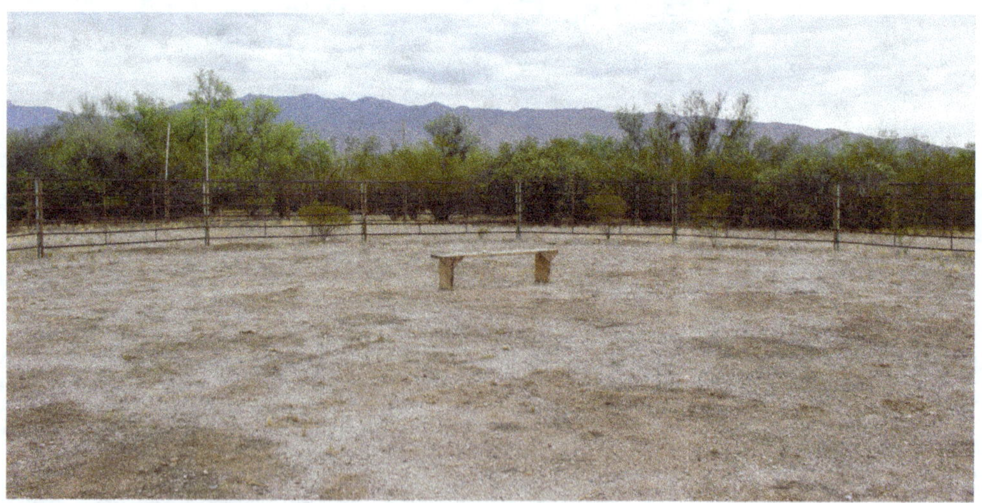

The corral cleared of desert broom and other plants. Our tabula rasa.

had many large trash bags of desert broom and mesquite and had to rent a 50-foot U-Haul truck to take all those plants away to the local mulching facility.

What we had left was a large circle of relatively flat and dry land, pebbled with the tiny stones that are everywhere in the Sonoran Desert and give much of the land here a look similar to a spread of fresh kitty litter.

It was lovely to stand and contemplate this blank slate. It was up to us to build on it a structure worthy of the land.

We felt we were up to the task.

Acquiring the Tools

This wasn't exactly our first labyrinth. Once on the Oregon coast, we drew a temporary labyrinth in the beach sand with a stick. It was, of course, washed away in the next tide.

We also once made a small labyrinth by laying out a long rope in the grass next to our Washington house. That one didn't last very long either.

But this one on the Sanctuary was going to be different. We wanted it to be permanent, and we intended it to be a feature of the Sanctuary that people would want to come to and walk.

In other words, we needed it to look good. We wanted our measurements to be precise, our arcs to be smooth and pleasing to the eye, and our path widths uniform.

As we went through the process, we discovered things we needed that we didn't expect. Things like pads for our knees so that when we were kneeling to place rocks, we would preserve our joints from damage. An obvious consideration now, but it had not occurred to us when we started.

The following is a list of items we consider essential if you want to construct a labyrinth using rocks on bare ground.

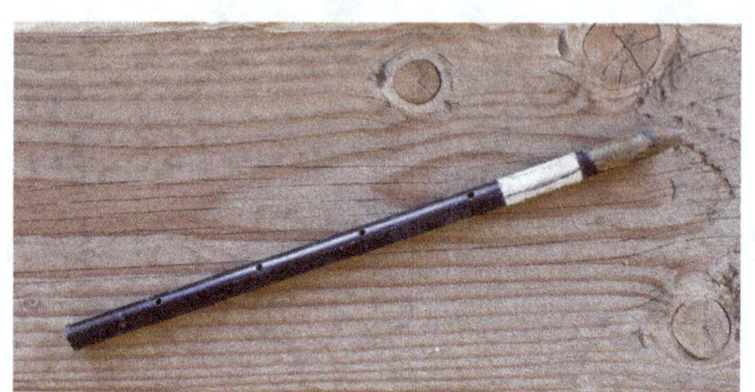

A metal stake to be hammered into the ground at the center of your labyrinth.

1. A stake. You will pound this into the ground at the center of the labyrinth. It will be the anchor of most of your measurements and most of your drawings. Make it strong. We bought a metal one about 2 feet long and hammered it a good foot into the ground so that it did not wobble even a fraction of an inch.

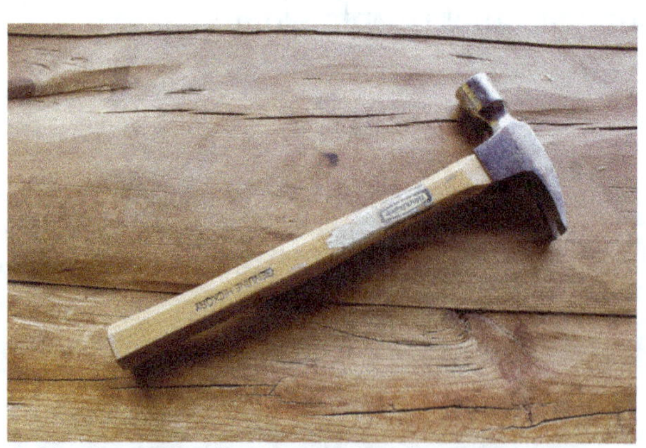

A fine hammer for hammering the stake into the ground.

2. A hammer. Use this to hammer in the stake.

3. Measuring tape. It should be metal, and it should be longer than the radius of your biggest circle.

Our labyrinth was 50 feet in diameter, so we needed a measuring tape at least 25 feet long.

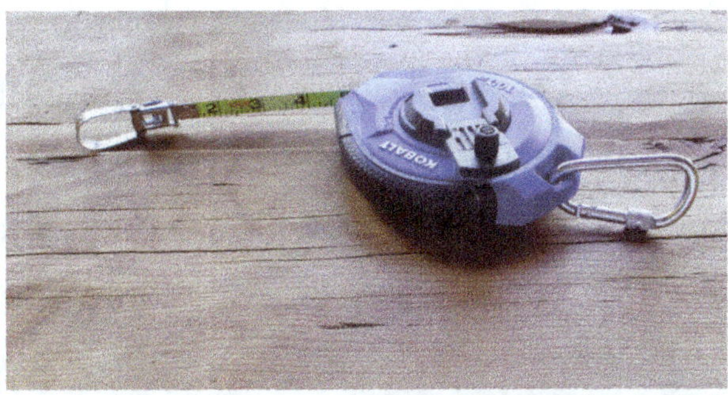

A good metal tape measure. Extremely useful for all your labyrinth measurements.

The one we got had a little metal loop at the zero mark, which was also very useful as it looped around the center stake and stayed in place. We highly recommend you get one with this feature.

4. Knee pads. You can get ones that wrap around each of your knees, or you can get a cushiony pad that you can move around the labyrinth as you work. We bought pairs of the ones that go on your knees, but we found them uncomfortable and bruising, so we took them back and used the pads instead. Here's a picture of them. They worked just fine.

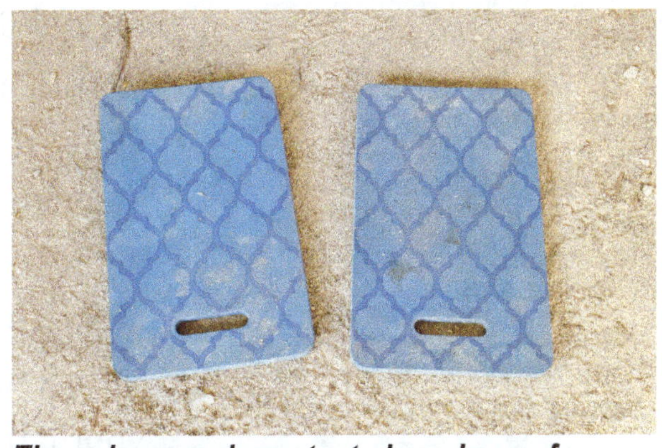

These knee pads protected our knees from discomfort and injury.

5. Wooden dowel. It should be fairly long and sturdy. About 5 feet or so in length and probably best to be at least half an inch thick. You will use this to draw your circles and lines. It is much more comfortable to draw from a standing position rather than a crouched or kneeling position, hence the length requirement.

6. A diagram of a completed labyrinth. You can use the one at the end of this book. We put it on a separate page so you can copy it or tear or cut it out. It might be a good idea to laminate it. That's what we did. We constantly referred to our diagram throughout the building process and were glad to have a sturdy one that didn't tear or get blown away by the wind.

7. Rope. It should be at least a little longer than the diameter of your labyrinth. It will most likely stretch a little, but that doesn't matter. We used the rope to help draw the straight lines that form the foundation of the labyrinth.

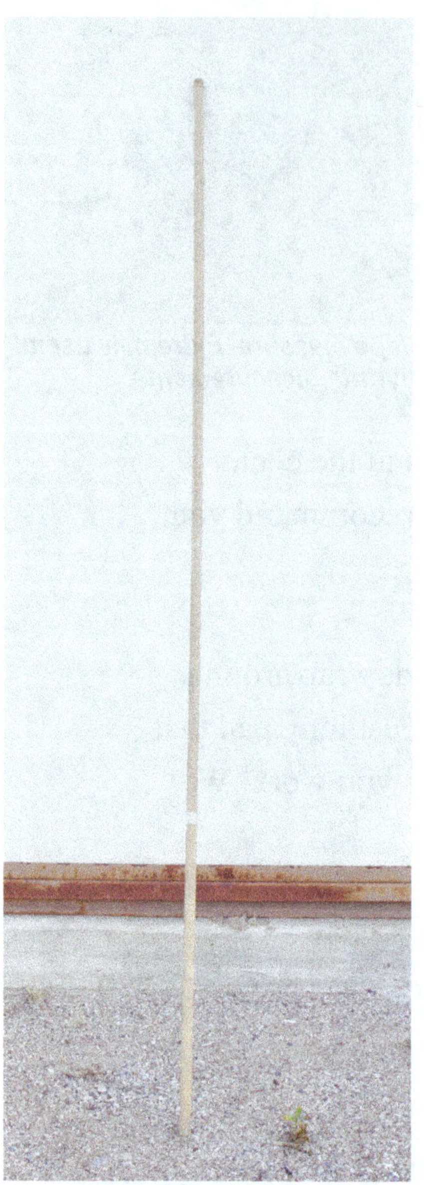

A sturdy wooden dowel for drawing the labyrinth circles.

8. Dust masks. We were in close proximity to the dirt much of the time, and we kicked up dust as we moved rocks, drew lines, and placed rocks on the ground. It's always best practice to protect your lungs.

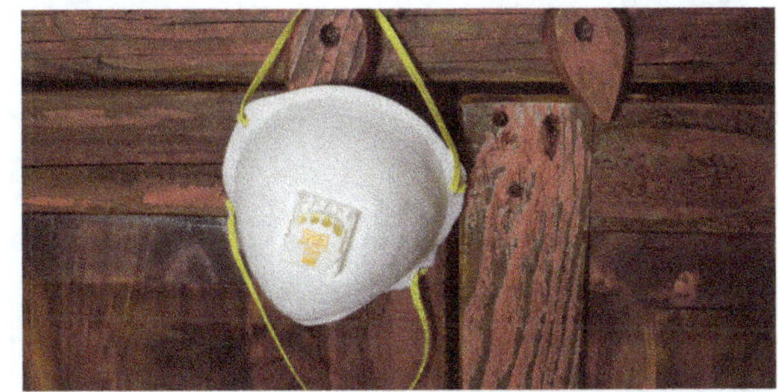

Save your lungs! Use a dust mask.

9. Work gloves. Perhaps not absolutely necessary, but we were glad for them, especially after handling hundreds of rough rocks in the gritty dirt.

10. Wheelbarrow. Again, not absolutely necessary, but it made moving the rocks around the perimeter of the labyrinth preparatory to placing

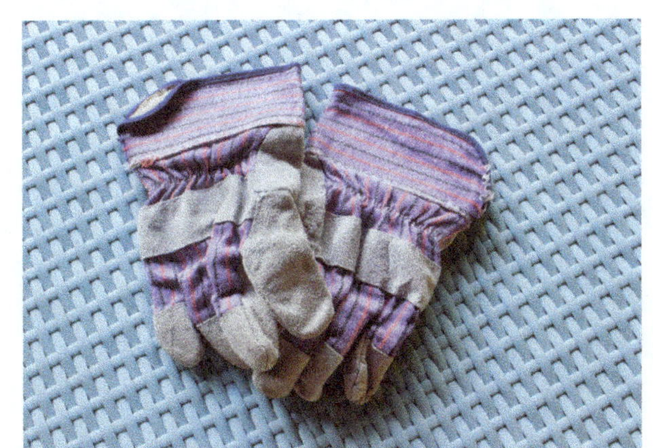

Save your hands! Use work gloves

them on our drawn lines much easier. You could also use a bucket to move rocks from place to place.

Acquiring the Rocks

We had a lot of discussion about rocks. What size, what color, what texture, and so on. We bought a bag of rocks from a home improvement store. They were uniform and pleasing to the eye, with a color and shape that made them look like a sack of potatoes. We laid out a line of these rocks in the dirt. After mea-

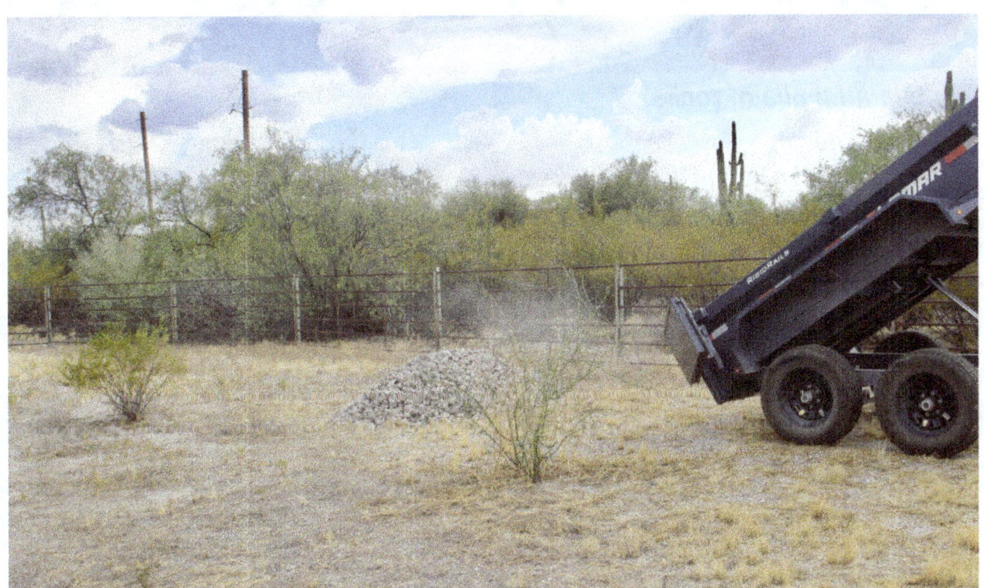

Our rocks delivered by dump truck near the future site of our labyrinth.

suring the length of the line, we determined that getting enough bags of these rocks to complete our labyrinth would cost well over $500. We weren't prepared to spend that much, so we investigated some alternatives.

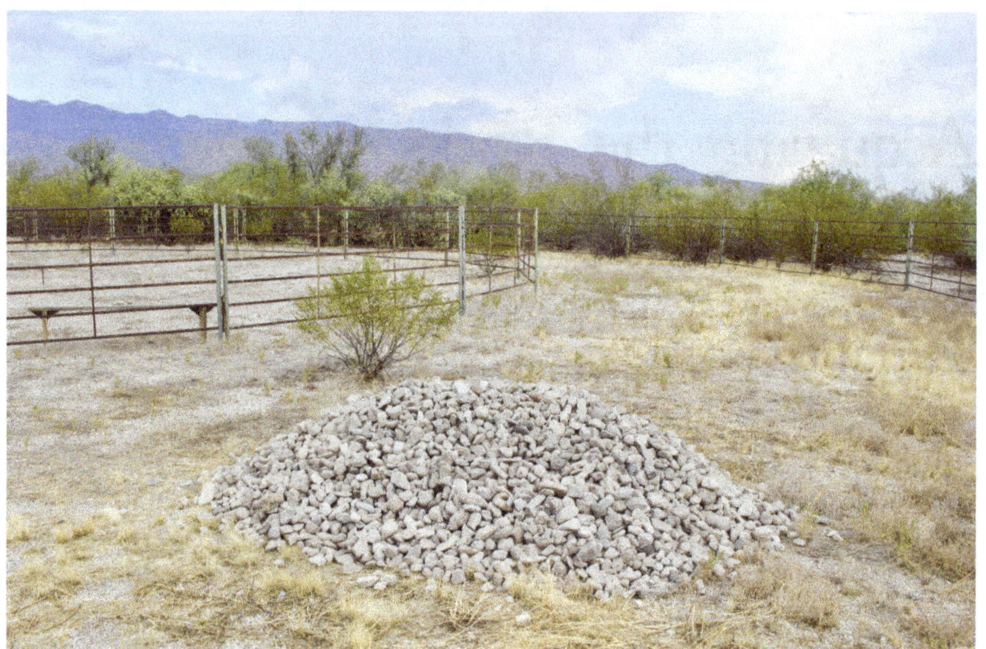
Our beautiful pile of rocks.

We went to a sand and gravel place and looked around at their offerings. We found a wide variation in rock size, texture, color, and price. We settled on rocks that they got from a nearby wash. They were mostly between two and four inches in diameter, and we could get a ton of them for $30, which was much more agreeable to our budget. Delivery to the corral was another $60.

We thought a ton was probably enough, but just to be sure we bought a ton and a half.

The man who delivered them put them exactly where we wanted them, which was about ten feet from the corral. Our plan was to load up our wheelbarrow with rocks and move them to convenient places around the perimeter of the labyrinth from where we would place the rocks.

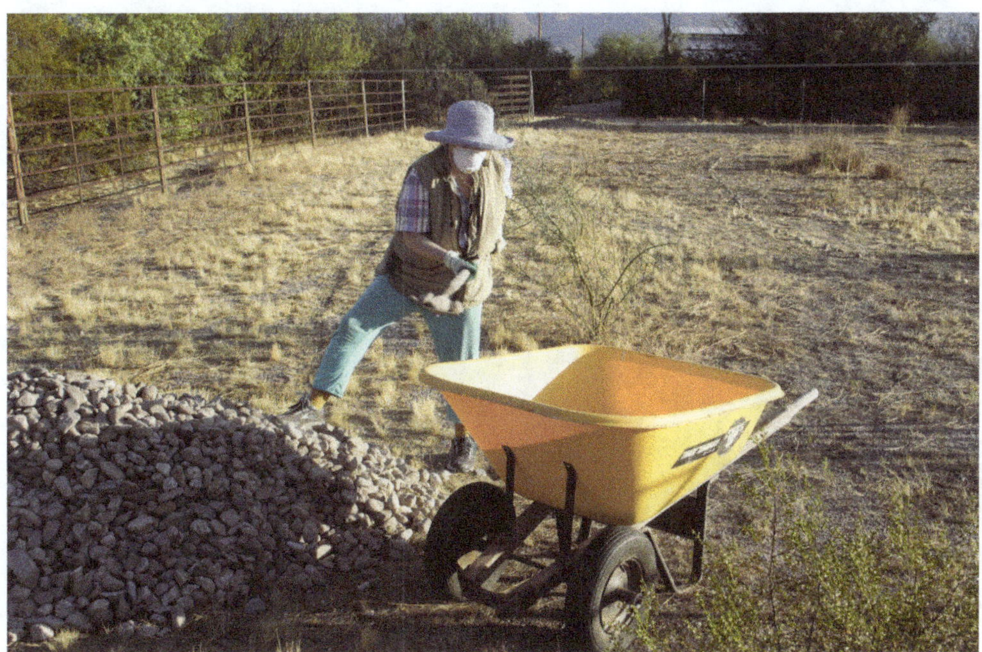

Kim loading rocks into our trusty wheelbarrow.

Calculating the Dimensions

We will describe our calculations for our particular labyrinth, but you should modify your calculations for the size of your labyrinth.

But first, let's take a look at the diagram of the Chartres labyrinth.

Notice that the paths are indicated in white, and the lines where the rocks will go are shown in black.

There is one path that takes you from the entrance to the center, and this same path takes you from the center back to the entrance. The entrance is at the bottom, slightly to the

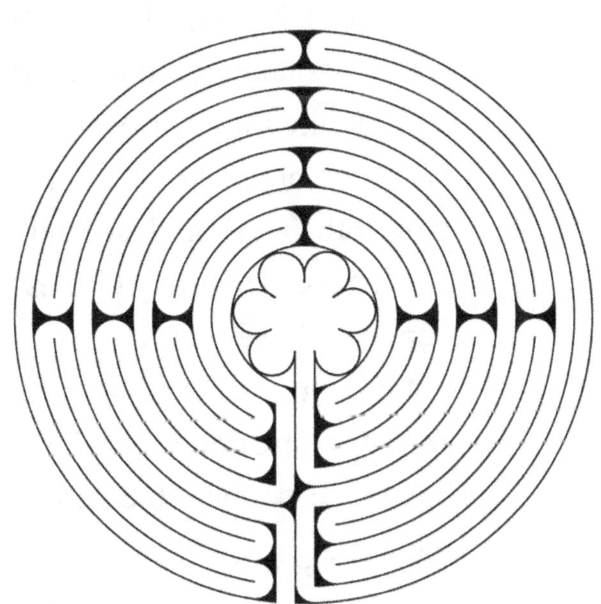

The design of the Chartres labyrinth.

left of center. This off-center aspect of labyrinths gives it a hint of rebelliousness, a bit of dynamic appeal.

The one-way-in-and-one-way-out feature is the distinguishing characteristic of a modern labyrinth. Unlike a maze, where there may be many paths, a labyrinth does not try to get you to take false turns or go down dead ends. It's a meditative experience rather than a trickster experience.

Our enclosure was 60 feet in diameter. We decided on a labyrinth 50 feet in diameter. This would give a five-foot wide path between the fence of the enclosure and the edge of the labyrinth. It felt like a nice fit, and it would give us room to put a bench or two around the perimeter of the labyrinth.

Our labyrinth is an 11-circuit version, like the Chartres labyrinth. This means there are 11 circular paths that take you through the labyrinth.

To make those 11 paths requires you to draw 12 circles. The biggest circle will be the diameter of the labyrinth. The smallest circle will define the center, and all the remaining circles will be spread out evenly between those two.

Of course, the paths are not complete circuits, despite the 11-circuit name. The paths twist and turn and have places where they are blocked off and where there are gaps, but for purposes of understanding the structure of the labyrinth, keep those 11 circuits and 12 circles in mind.

The diameter of the center of the labyrinth is one quarter the diameter of the entire labyrinth. For our labyrinth, the center is therefore 12.5 feet in diameter, which is a radius of 6.25 feet, or 6 feet and 3 inches.

To determine the width of our paths, we need to divide the remaining radius by 11 (since this is an 11-circuit labyrinth). 25 feet minus 6.25 feet gives us 18.75 feet. Divide 18.75 by 11 to get 1.7 feet, which is 20.46 inches. To make the measuring easier we rounded this up to get 20.5 inches as the width of our path.

We need to draw 12 circles 20.5 inches apart.

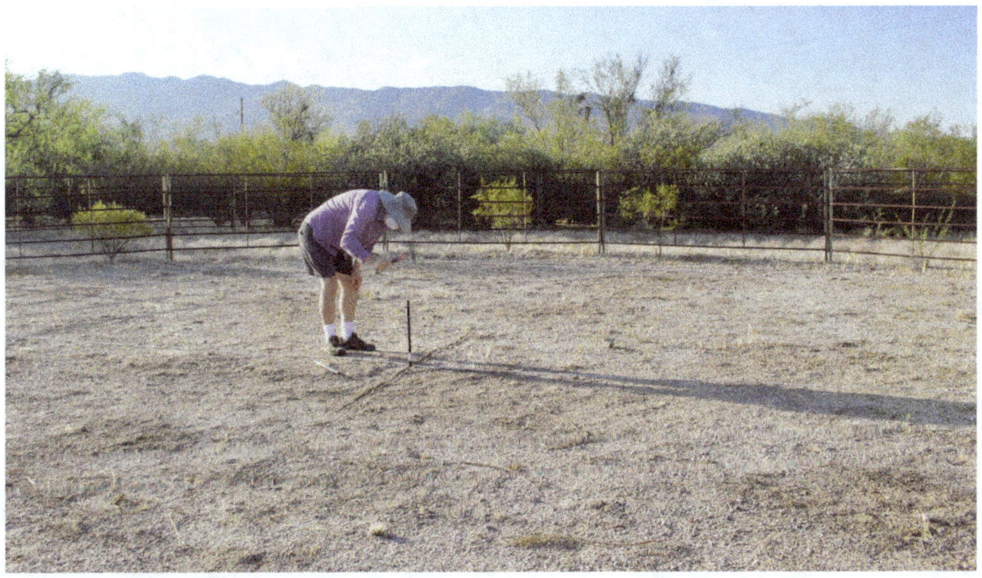

Mario hammers in the center stake.

If you are more comfortable with a formula, use this one:

$$W = .0682r$$

where W is the WIDTH of your paths, and r is the RADIUS of your labyrinth.

This is an important number. It determines the placement of each circle you will be drawing.

Once you have the width of your path determined, it is time to start drawing your labyrinth for real, in the dirt.

Drawing the Labyrinth

First, locate the center of your labyrinth. We determined our center by stretching a rope from one edge of the corral to the opposite edge. We drew a line in the dirt at about the center mark of the rope, then moved the rope to approximately 90 degrees to the first line, stretched it out, and marked the spot where the rope intersected the first line we had drawn.

This was our center point.

We hammered our stake into this spot.

You can also find the center by eye. If you do, it might be a good idea to measure a few radius lengths out from your center point to make sure the labyrinth will be situated exactly where you want it to be.

In the diagrams that follow, lines in **red** will indicate the most recently drawn lines.

Lines and areas in **black** will be where you should place rocks.

Items in **green** are areas you draw, but do not place rocks upon.

Items in **blue** show line segments that need to be measured. Do not place rocks on these lines.

For example, in Diagram 1, below, the center stake is indicated by red. In the next diagram it will be green, since no rock is placed on it.

Diagram 1. The center stake. The beginning of the labyrinth.

Drawing the First Circle

Hook your tape measure onto the center stake. Measure out the radius of your labyrinth. In our case, the radius was 25 feet. We used masking tape to tape the dowel to the 25-foot mark of the tape measure. Make sure the measuring tape is close to the ground. We recommend it be no more than a couple of inches from the ground. Any higher, and your circle might not be as accurate as it should be.

Now, hold the dowel in both hands, pull the measuring tape taut, and put the end of the dowel into the dirt. While keeping the measuring tape taut and the dowel straight up and down, drag the end of the dowel in the dirt. It will naturally draw a circle. (See Diagram 2.) Work slowly, especially if the ground is at all hilly or uneven.

There is no need to gouge a deep valley as you draw. You don't need to go much deeper than a quarter-inch or so. You are making a space for the rocks, not digging a trench. You only need a line to indicate where to place the rocks.

You may wonder why we didn't use a rope to draw the circles. Good question. We tried that first but found that the rope stretched, which made for inaccurate circles. We did not have that problem with the metal measuring tape.

Diagram 2. The first circle. This circle is the size of the completed labyrinth.

Placing the Rocks

There are two schools of thought on rock placing.

The first method is to draw the labyrinth completely, then place the rocks. The second method is to place rocks as each circle is done.

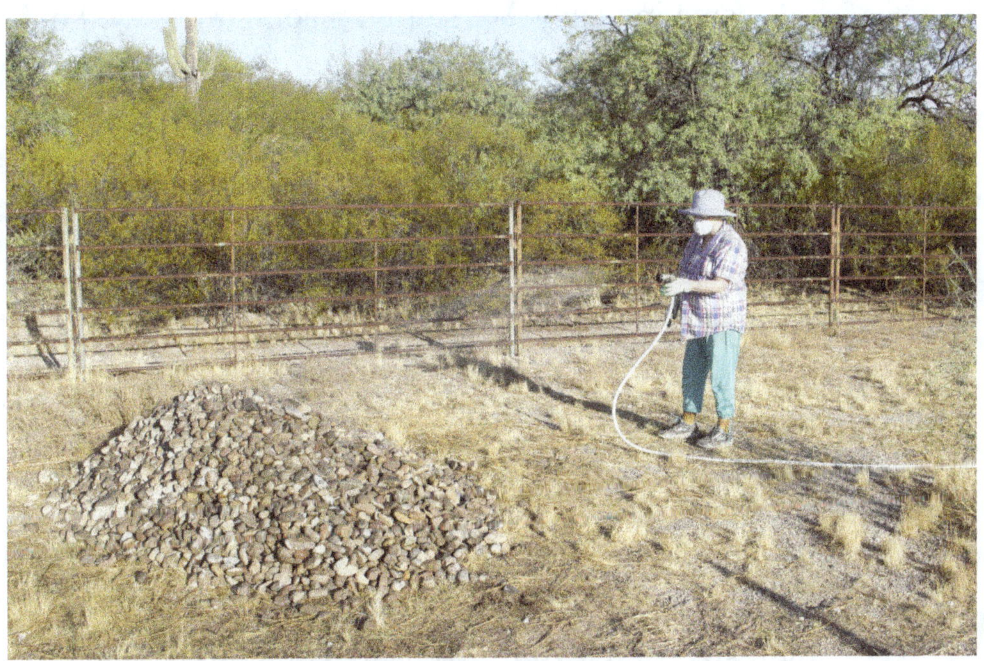

Kim hoses down the rocks to help cut down on dust.

Which method you choose is up to you. We decided to place our rocks as we drew each circle. Our thought was that if we drew the entire labyrinth first, parts of it might deteriorate due to weather, animal activity, or our own feet before we could place all the rocks, and we would have to redraw some of the labyrinth. Not a huge problem, since it is easy to redraw a circle if necessary, but one we chose to avoid.

For the remainder of these instructions, we're going to proceed by the second method, placing rocks as each circle is done, but do go with your gut here. There is no right or wrong way to do this.

So, once you have your first circle, place your rocks.

This is where our wheelbarrow, gloves, and knee pads came in handy. We started placing rocks without the knee pads, but that didn't last. It is painful and annoying to kneel on gravel! We quickly took refuge in our portable knee pads.

Load up your wheelbarrow (or bucket) with rocks and move them to locations around the big circle you drew. Place the rocks on the circle. (This isn't rocket science!)

We found that this part of the process was almost as meditative as ultimately walking the labyrinth. We were building the labyrinth, stone by stone. No hurrying. It settled our minds. Each rock had its own shape, color, size, and texture. We were communing with

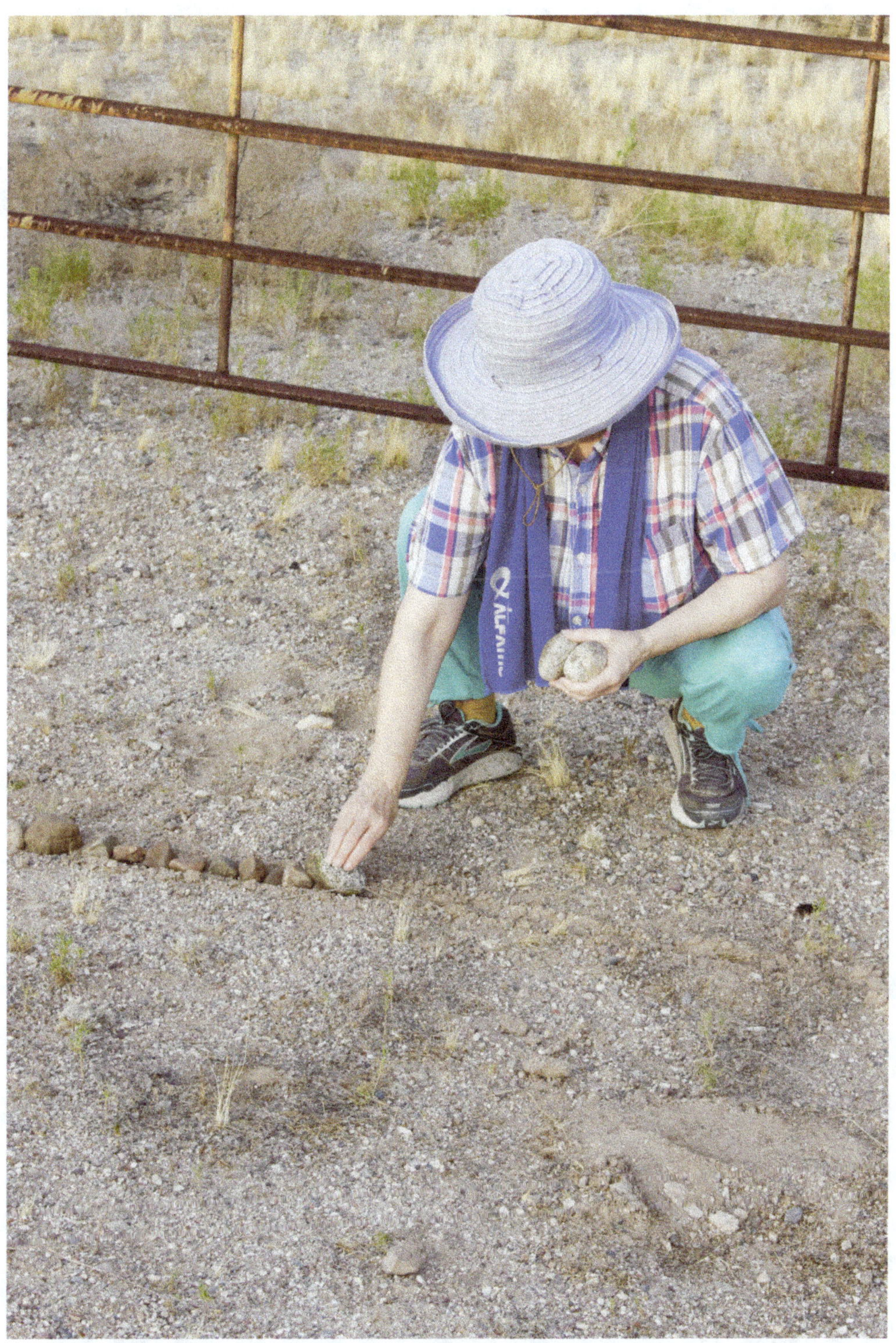

The act of placing rocks brings meditative peace and joy.

them as we placed them. The rocks kissed each other along the circle we had drawn.

It was a lovely part of the construction and would remain so throughout the process. There was always a little jolt of excitement as we placed a stone that completed a circle, or a turn, or a termination in a circle.

So do take time to admire your first circle once it is done. The pleasure of admiring a job well done (and all the mini-jobs in-between) is always a benefit of any project such as this one.

Location, Location, Location (again)

Now that you have the big circle drawn and filled in with rocks, you need to decide the location of the entrance to your labyrinth.

Do you want to face the rising sun in the morning when you walk your labyrinth? If so, place your entrance accordingly.

Or maybe you want the light of the setting sun on your face when you walk your labyrinth in the evening?

Or perhaps there's a nearby landmark you would like to face as you begin your walk. Spend some time wandering the space you have set aside for your labyrinth. The orientation of your labyrinth is a personal choice, one that will determine some of the character of your labyrinth. Take your time so your choice is one you are happy with. It will enhance the experience of walking your labyrinth.

After much consideration, we decided to place our entrance so that we would be facing the Rincon Mountains, and we would see the sun rising in the morning. Given the hot days in the Sonoran desert, we figured a lot of our labyrinth walking would be in the relative cool of the morning, and seeing the sun come up over the Rincon Mountains as we prepared to walk the path would be a pleasing experience.

A Bit of Clarification

We're going to get down into the nitty-gritty of the structure of the labyrinth as we go on from here, so some common points of reference will help you understand our instructions better.

Take a look at your laminated diagram, and let's give the diagram directions. The entrance we'll call S (south). The opposite side will be N (north). The left W (west) and the right E (east). We'll use these terms when referring to parts of the labyrinth even if in the real world your labyrinth is not situated in a north/south orientation.

Let's also refer to the quadrants by the directional terms, so that we will have a NE quadrant to the upper right, a SE quadrant to the lower right, a SW quadrant to the lower left, and a NW quadrant to the upper left.

You may want to mark your diagram with a sharpie to keep things straight.

Onward.

Drawing the Cross

Examine your laminated copy of the Chartres labyrinth. Note the structure. There are, as we have indicated, 11 paths, which means 12 circles. Ignore the center for now. We will deal with those details in a future section. The circles have what we call decision points. These are places where the circle either stops or keeps going. For each circle, there are four such decision points, or four places where the circle either breaks or does not.

These decision points are situated on a cross that is made up of a N/S line and, at right angles, a W/E line.

Your next task is to draw this cross.

To do this, begin by stretching your rope from the south edge of the big circle, through the center, to the north edge of the big circle.

Now you need to draw the line that the rope defines. We found the best way to do this was to keep the rope taut and carefully walk on the length of it, with no space between your steps, so that an impression of the rope transfers to the dirt. Once you have walked the length of the rope, remove it, and you will see a perfectly straight line in the dirt from one edge of the labyrinth to the other.

Next you will need to draw a line at right angles to this one, that is, along the west/east line. Here you can use your eye to locate the points on the big circle from which to draw your line, or you can employ the Pythagorean theorem to find the spot. (And you thought all that high school algebra would never be useful.) The length you are looking for, derived from the Pythagorean theorem, is given by the following formula:

$$L = 1.414r$$

where L is the length from the south entrance of the labyrinth to the east point on the circle, and also from the south entrance to the west point on the circle, and r is the radius of the circle.

In our case, L was 1.414 times 25, or 35.35.

From the south entrance, measure L feet toward the east edge and mark the spot. Then measure L feet to the west edge and mark that spot.

Now use your rope to draw the W/E line through the center that connects these two intersection points. This is the other line of the cross. (See Diagram 3.)

Place rocks along this line, leaving the center
(about a quarter of the length of the radius) empty.
Also, place rocks on the north side of the N/S line, but
not on the south side. The south side of the N/S line
does not define a rock line, but is, instead, the center
of the path that will ultimately take you into the center
of the labyrinth. (See Diagram 4.)

Also note that in the final labyrinth these lines will
be broken in places to allow some of the circles to go
through unimpeded. We will get to that later.

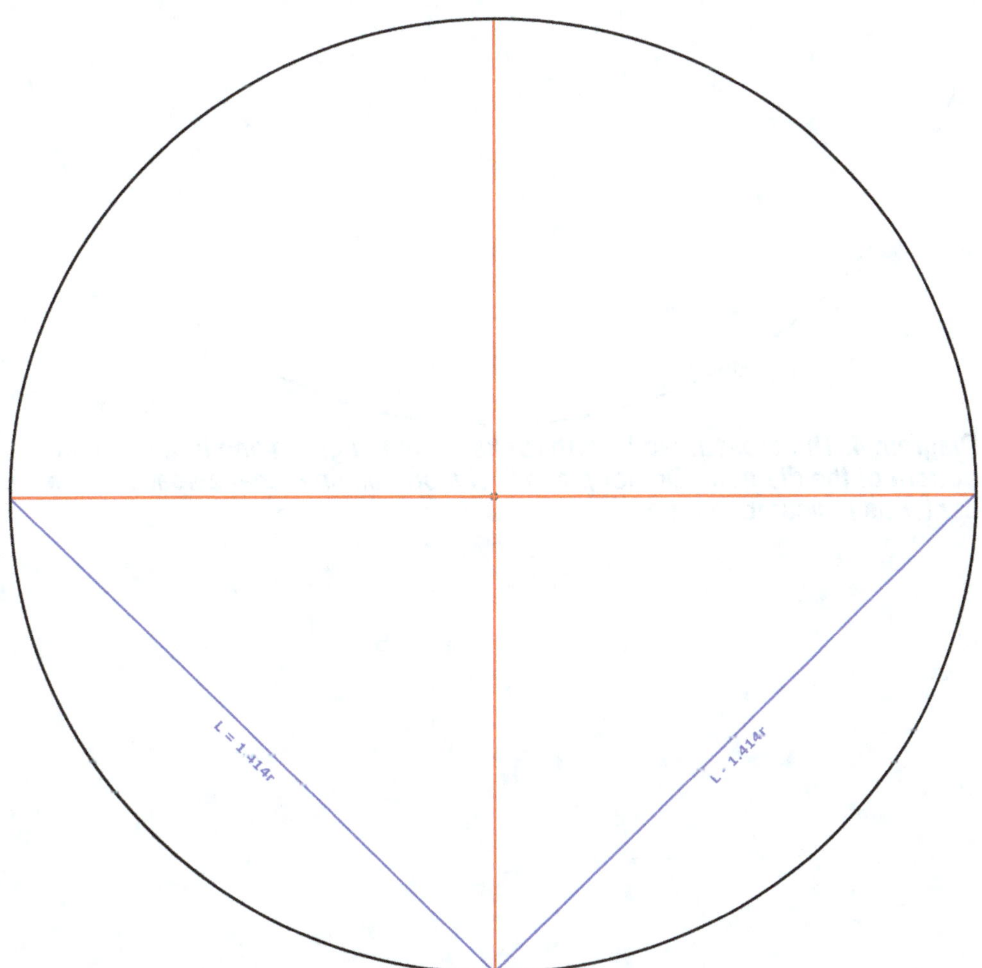

Diagram 3. The cross. This is the foundation of the labyrinth.

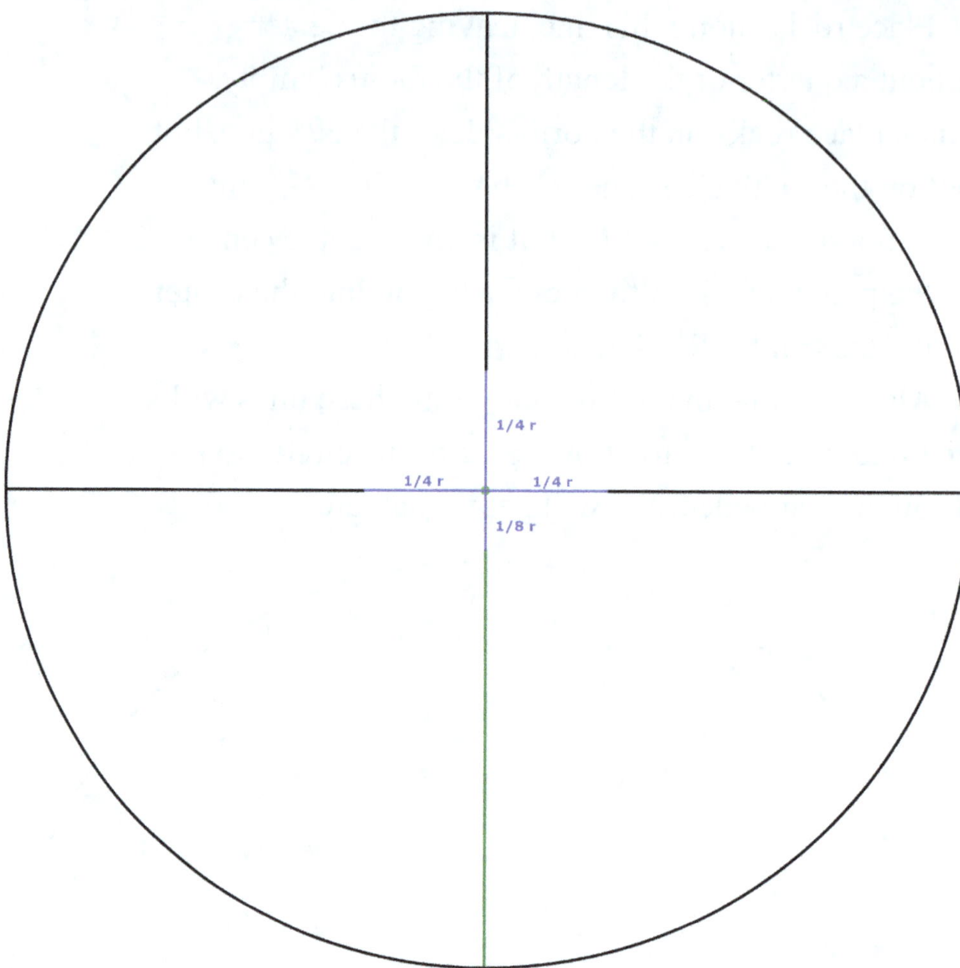

Diagram 4. The cross filled in with rocks. Note the green line in the center bottom of the diagram. Do not place rocks on this line. Leave space in the center as indicated in blue.

Drawing the Exit and Entrance Lines

Again, refer to your laminated copy of the Chartres labyrinth. Notice that most of the labyrinth's lines are arcs, except for some straight lines in the south. We're now going to draw these straight lines.

Recall the value of W, the width of your paths. The unrocked south line you drew in the previous section will be the center of a path W inches wide. In our case, we calculated W to be 20.5 inches. This means we need to draw lines 10.25 inches on either side of the south line, as this will define a path 20.5 inches wide. Your value of W will depend on the size of your labyrinth, as we indicated in the previous chapter "Calculating the Dimensions." (Page 31.)

Use your tape measure to mark this distance at several points to the east of the south line. Then line up your rope on these points, stretch it taut, and walk on it to mark a straight line in the dirt. Do the same on the west side of the south line.

Place rocks on these two lines, but leave unrocked near the center stake a length approximately half the radius of the center.

Now you have one more straight line to draw. It is in the SW quadrant, parallel to the south line.

Measure W inches to the west of the line you drew

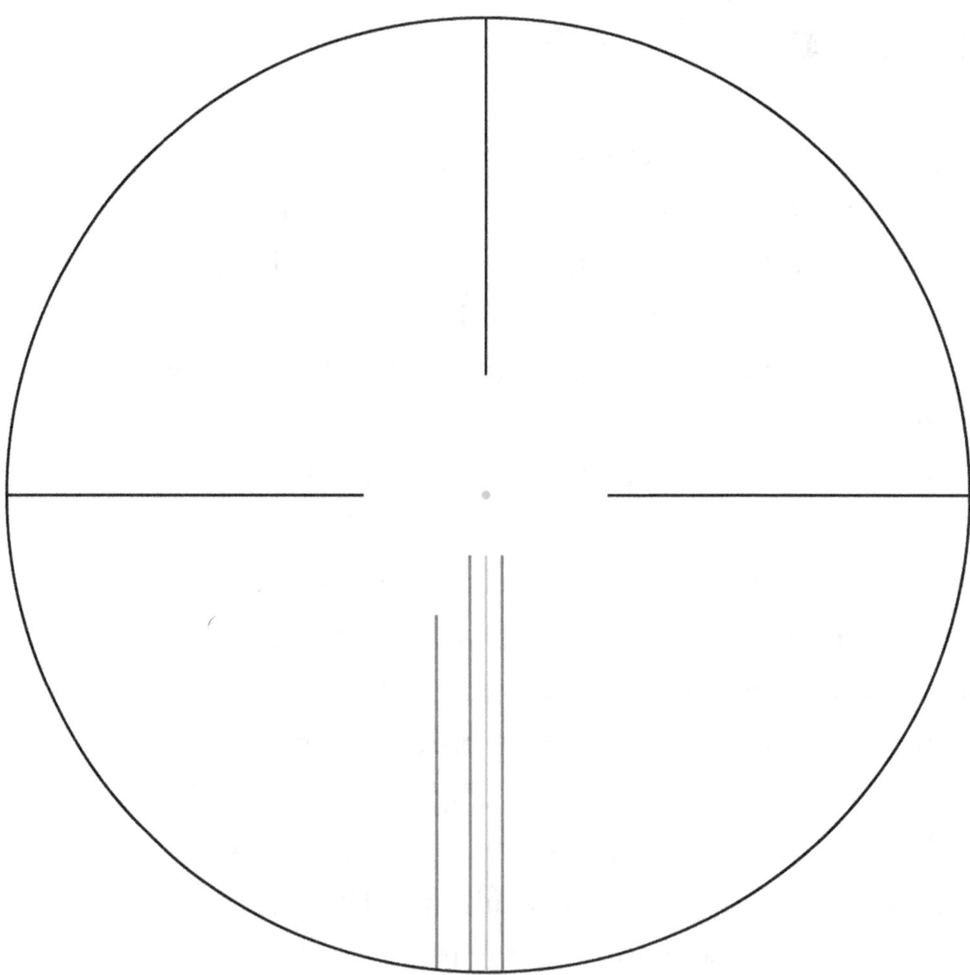

Diagram 5. The exit and entrance paths.

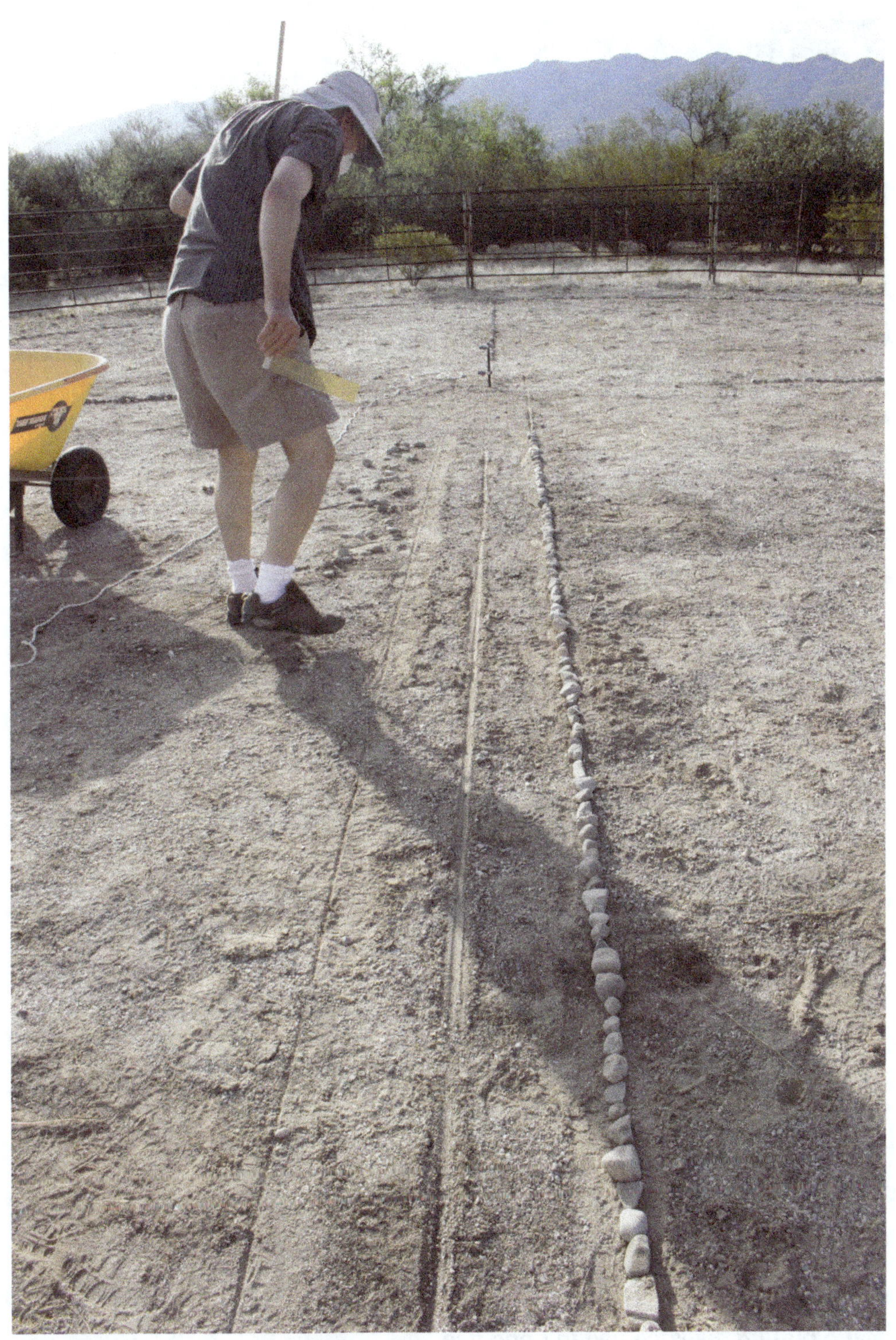

Drawing the exit and entrance paths.

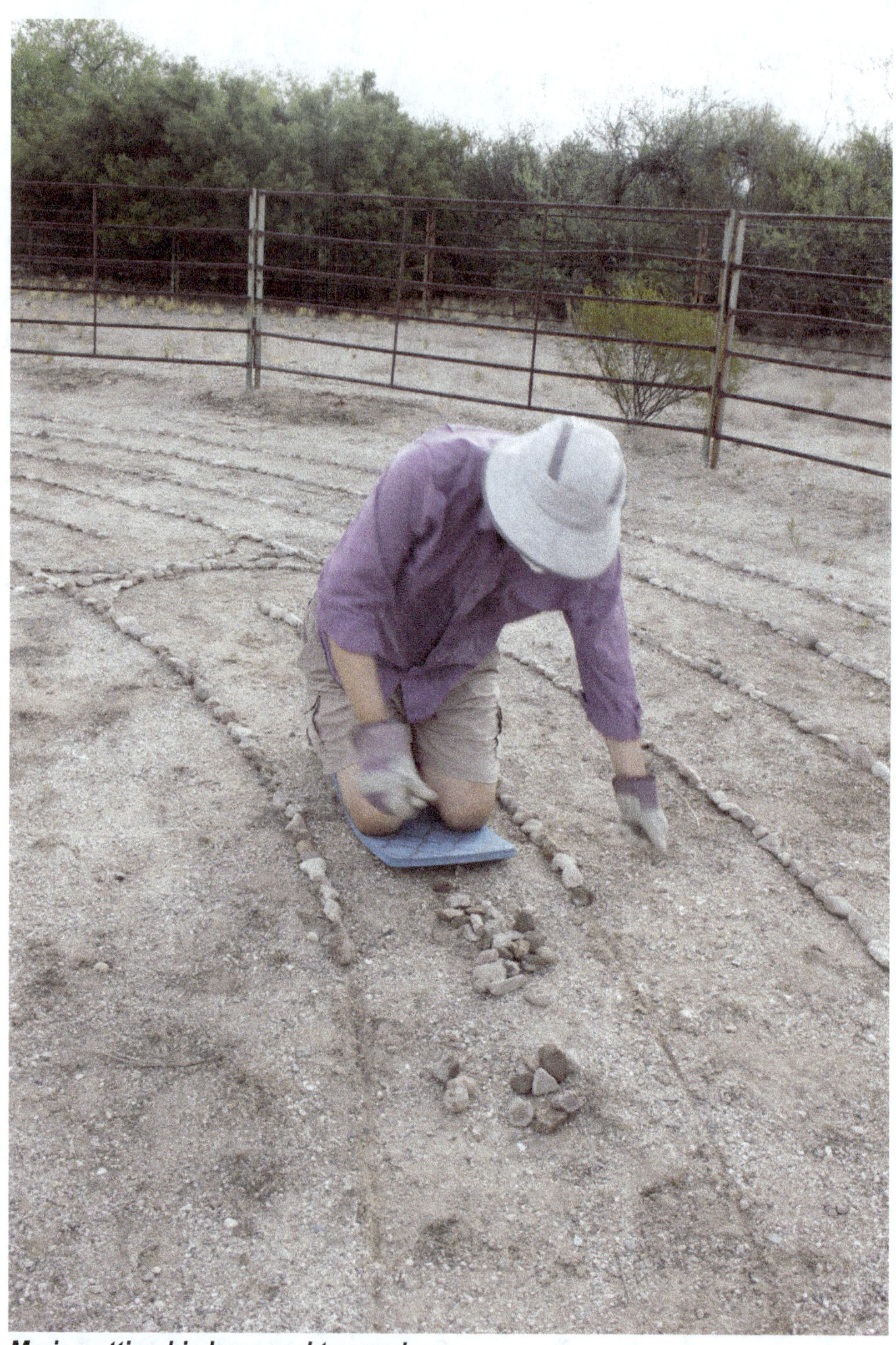

Mario putting his knee pad to good use.

to the west of the south line. As before, mark several points. Then use your rope, stretched taut, to walk on and define a straight line. Remove the rope and fill the line with rocks, leaving unrocked a length equal to a quarter of the radius of the labyrinth.

You should now have three parallel lines defining two straight paths. (See Diagram 5.) The path on the left will lead into and out of the labyrinth, and the path on the right will lead into and out of the center of the labyrinth.

Now is a good time to remove the rocks at the base of the left most path, opening the big circle. This will be where you enter your labyrinth.

In addition to the circle and the two ingress and egress paths, you should have a straight line on the north side of the center stake, and a straight line going east/west through the center stake.

(As you continue constructing your labyrinth, these lines will become line segments as you make room for the circles, but don't try to make these breaks just yet. It will be much more accurate to do the breaks as you draw the circles, and it will require less measuring.)

Take some time to admire the symmetry and the beauty of the arrangement. This is the skeleton of the labyrinth. On this structure we will add the twists and turns that transform these bare bones into a meandering life-like journey.

Drawing the Remaining Circles

Your next circle should be inside the big circle, separated from it by the width of your path. In our case, that was 20.5 inches.

We taped our dowel to the 23 feet 3.5 inch mark on our measuring tape and dragged the tip of the dowel in a circle around the center. Then we placed rocks on this circle.

We drew the next circle 20.5 inches inside this path, taping our dowel to the 21 feet 7 inch mark on the tape measure and placing rocks on it when it was finished. We continued in this manner until we had a total of 12 circles, including the first big circle. (See Diagram 6.)

As you proceed, each circle will, of course, be smaller than the one before. By the time you get to the last circle, it will be a quick task to draw the circle and place the rocks.

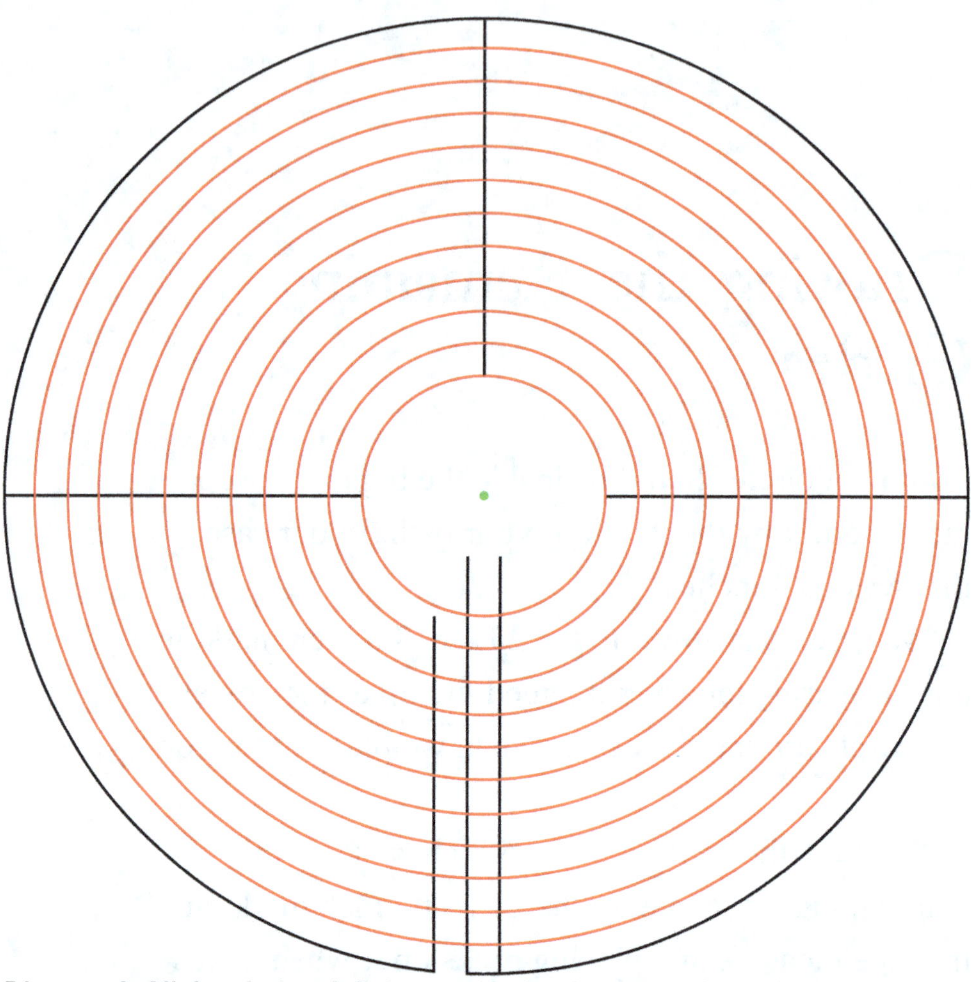

Diagram 6. All the circles defining an 11-circuit pattern. Note the rocks removed from the entrance at the bottom

Drawing the Breaks

Now step back and survey your labyrinth.

As we mentioned earlier, the circles in the completed labyrinth are not complete circles. They will sometimes be interrupted at the borders of the quadrants.

There is a pattern to these interruptions, and you can try to internalize these as you work, but the pattern is subtle and can be confusing since the labyrinth is a twisty path. We found the best way to identify the locations of the interruptions was to consult our laminated chart.

Use your chart to make sure you are creating breaks in the paths through the cross lines in the proper places.

Make your breaks W inches long, the width of your path, and remove the rocks at these breaks. (See Diagram 7.)

Once you have removed the rocks that define the

labyrinth's path, your labyrinth is more or less complete, except for the center, which we will take up next.

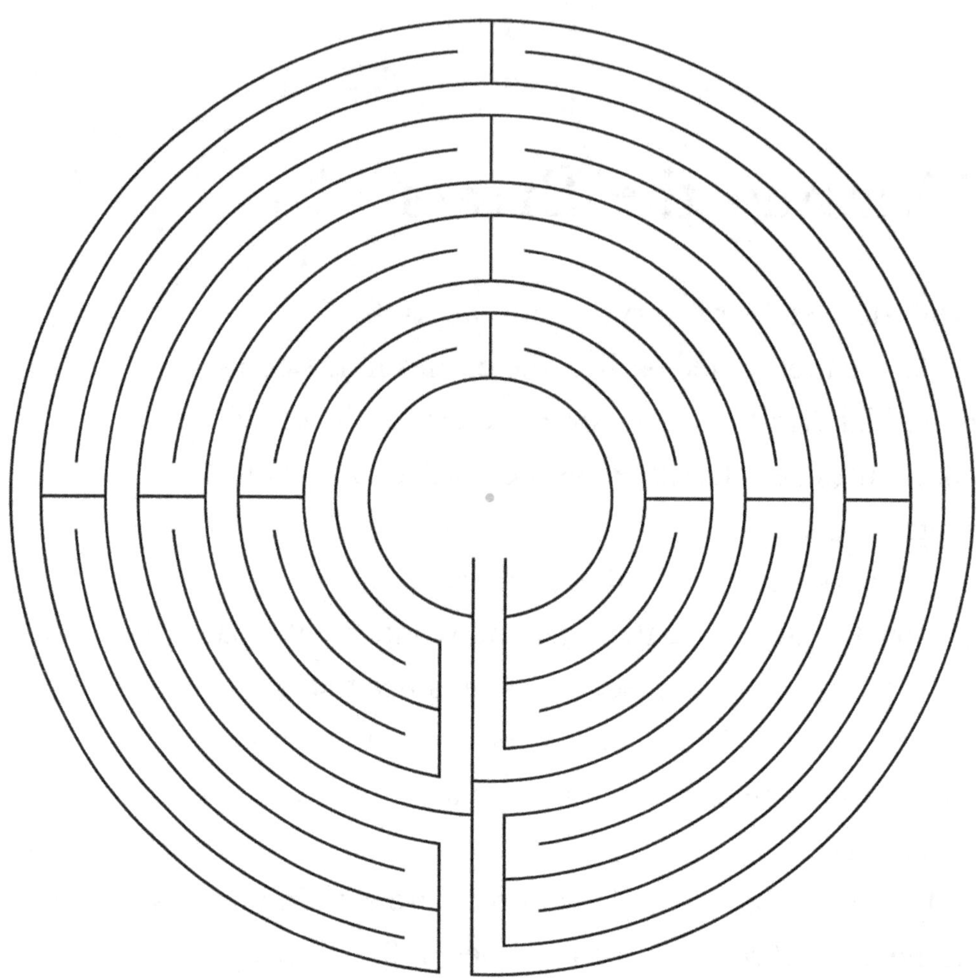

Diagram 7. All the circuits, with all the twists and turns. The labyrinth is now walkable.

Drawing the Center

The center is designed to look something like a flower. The path into the center resembles a stem, and the six loops arrayed around it are reminiscent of six petals.

You can draw these petals freehand, but we will attempt to outline a method below that is a little more rigorous and should result in a uniform set of petals.

To create the flower at the center of your labyrinth, begin by drawing a circle of radius equal to half the center. (See Diagram 8.)

In our case, the center radius was just a little over 6 feet, so we made the radius of this last circle 3 feet.

Once you have drawn this circle, remove the center stake. You don't need it anymore. If you leave it where it is, it may become a hazard as you work to create your six-petaled flower.

The path to the center should be W inches wide with two rows of rocks on both sides leading into the

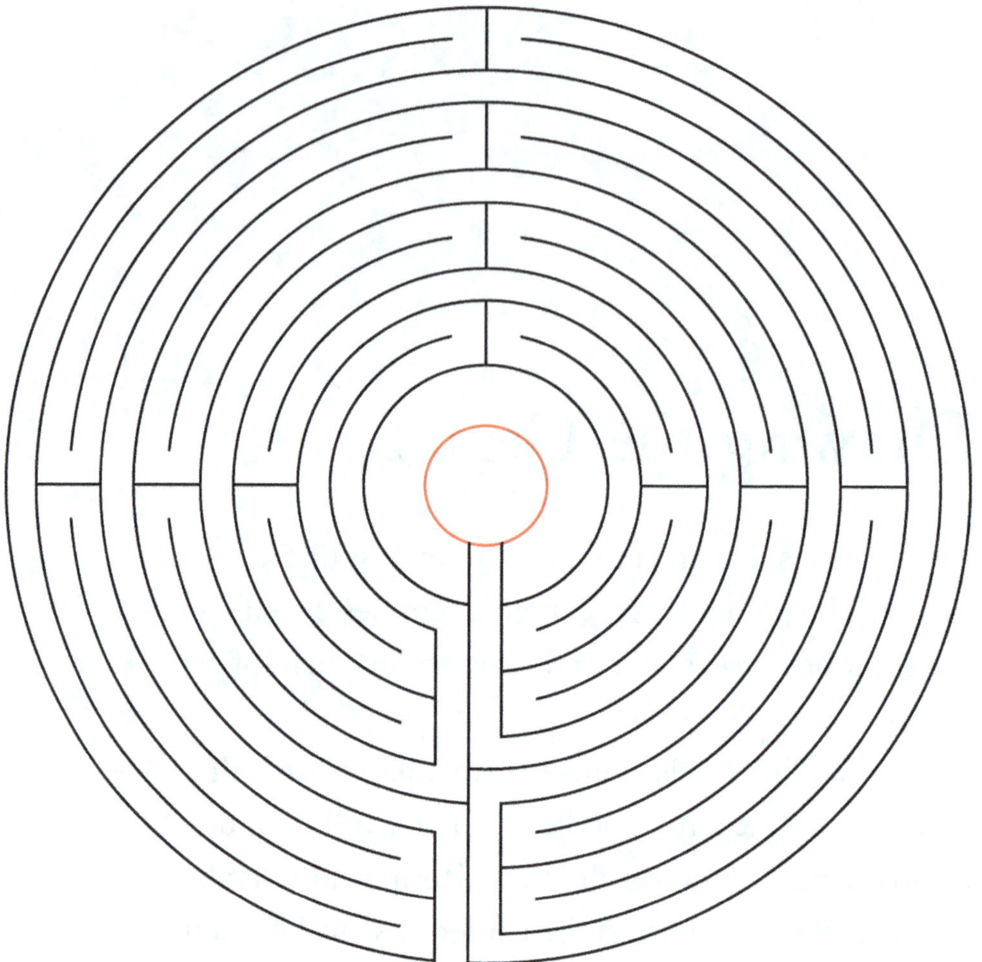

Diagram 8. The center circle is a guide to building the six-petalled flower.

center. If the two lines of the path don't end at the circle you just drew, add or remove rocks to these paths so that they do.

Consult your laminated diagram. Note that there are five more places on the last circle where the semi-circles of the petals terminate. To find these points you will need to do some measuring.

Recall the radius of your labyrinth. Multiply that

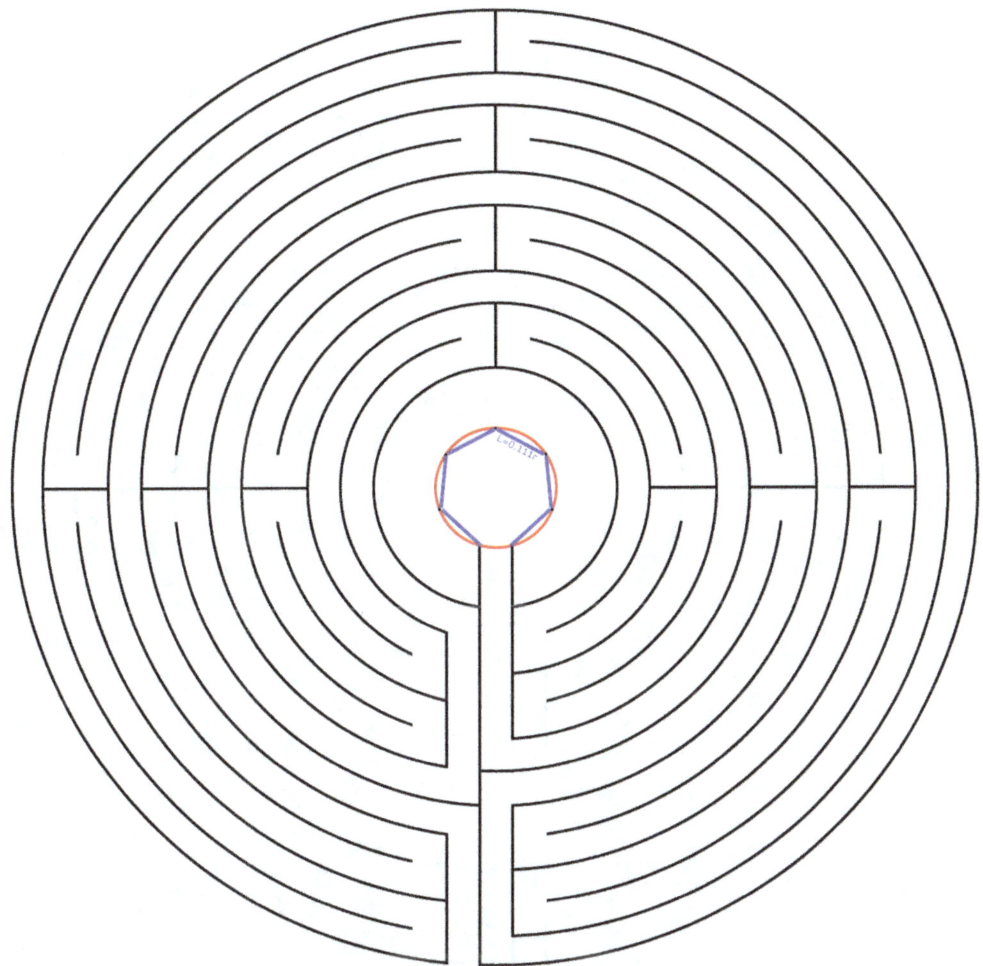

Diagram 9. Center measurements for the six-petalled flower.

figure by 0.111. This is the distance between the points where the petals meet. Measure along the final circle you drew and mark five points that will be 0.111r apart. (See Diagram 9.)

Place a rock at each of these points. (See Diagram 10.)

In our labyrinth, r was 300 inches. So, for us, 300 x

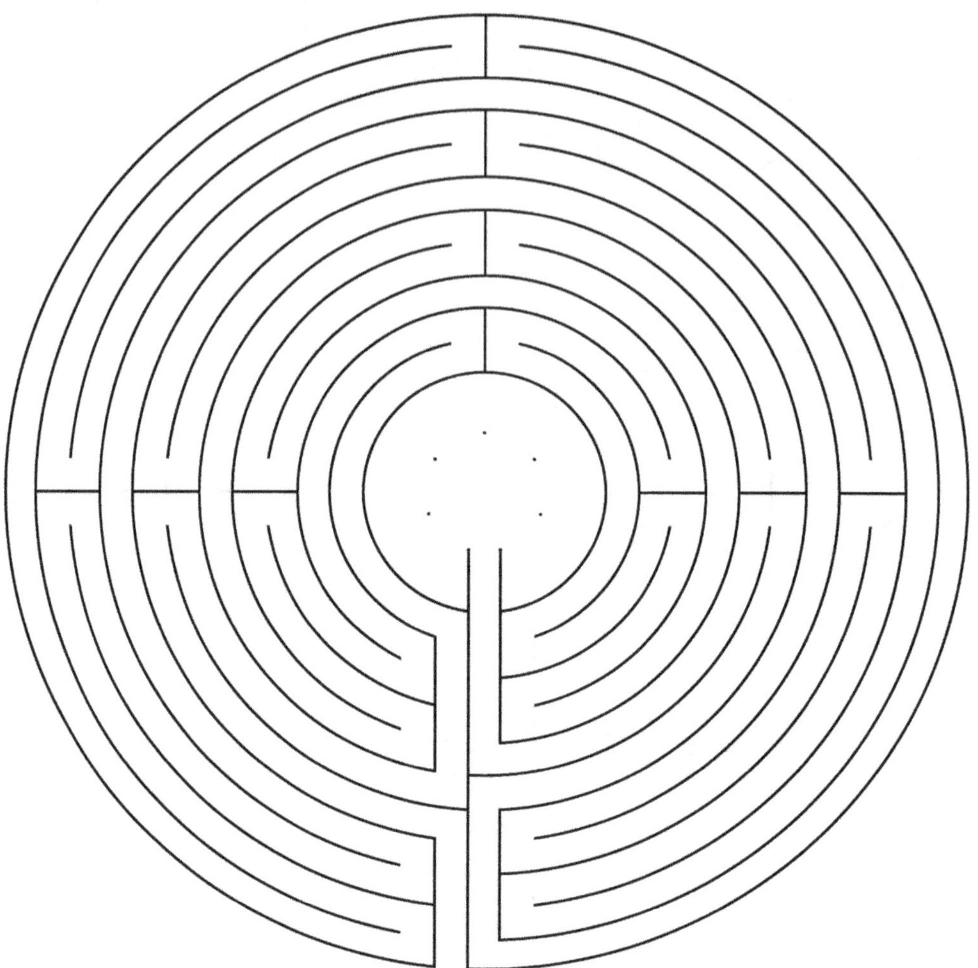

Diagram 10. The petals of the flower meet at the points in the center.

0.111 = 33.3 inches. Be sure to use your own value of r in your calculation.

Now that you have the points where the arcs of the petals meet, you need to draw the arcs.

At this stage, calculations seemed to fall apart for us. We tried drawing each of the circles, but could not figure out precisely where the centers of those circles should be. We tried drawing the petals freehand. This

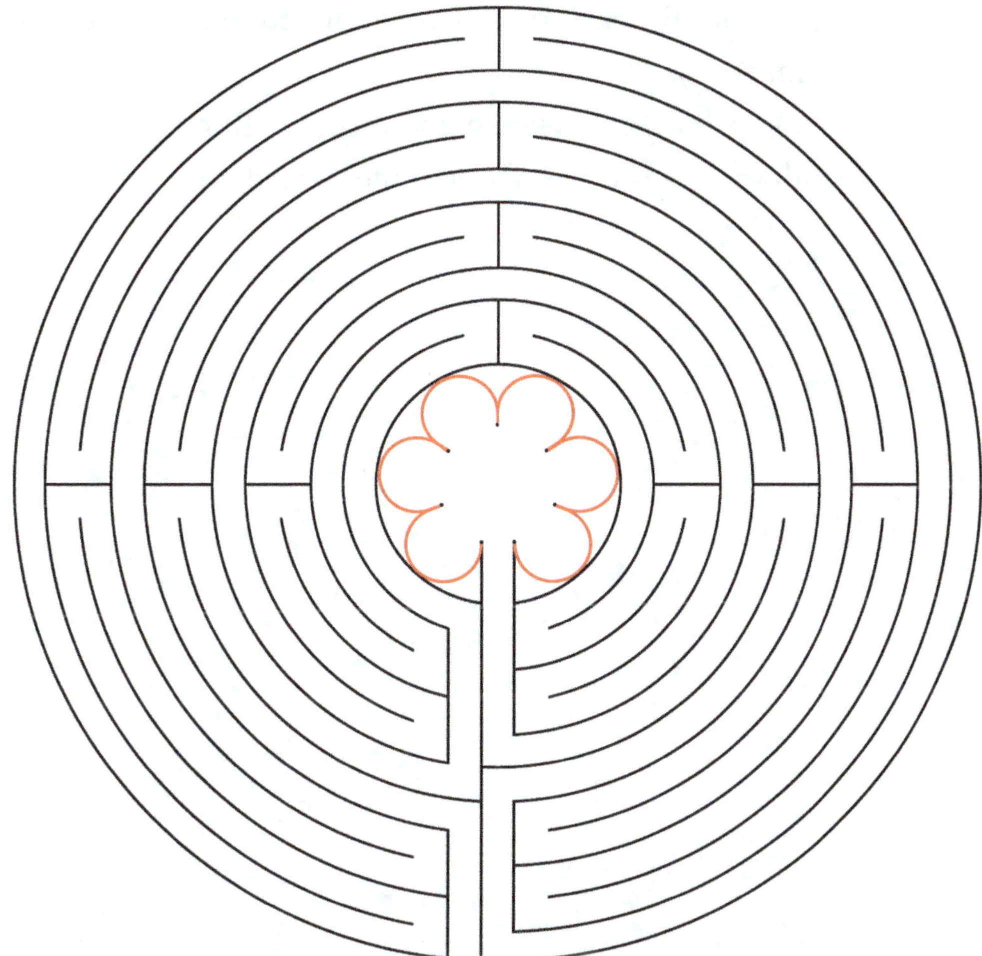

Diagram 11. Use the points in the previous diagram as guides to help you draw the semi-circular petals.

worked fairly well, but the arcs were not as precise as we wanted.

In the end, we traced out a circle on butcher paper, cut it out, and placed it in the spaces where the petals needed to be drawn, one petal at a time. Using the butcher paper circle as a guide, we were able to trace out a path for each petal with a gloved finger. (See Diagram 11.)

Once the paths were completed, we filled them in with rocks. And voila, our center was done.

Drawing the Curves

An attractive labyrinth has curves at the turns.

To make the curves, do the following:

Locate one of the places where a circle is broken. There should be a line perpendicular to the circle W inches away from it. Using your tape measure, mark off several spots W inches from the end of the circle so that you form a rough semi-circle. Connect these several spots. You can use a stick or a pen or pencil if you wish. We just used the tip of a gloved finger to draw the short path in the dirt.

Once you have this semi-circle, fill it in with rocks. Do this for all the places in the labyrinth where a circle breaks in front of a straight line. There are 28 such places. There are also a few places where you can smooth out a sharp turn with a curved row of rocks. There are 6 of these along the entrance and exit paths. (See Diagram 12.)

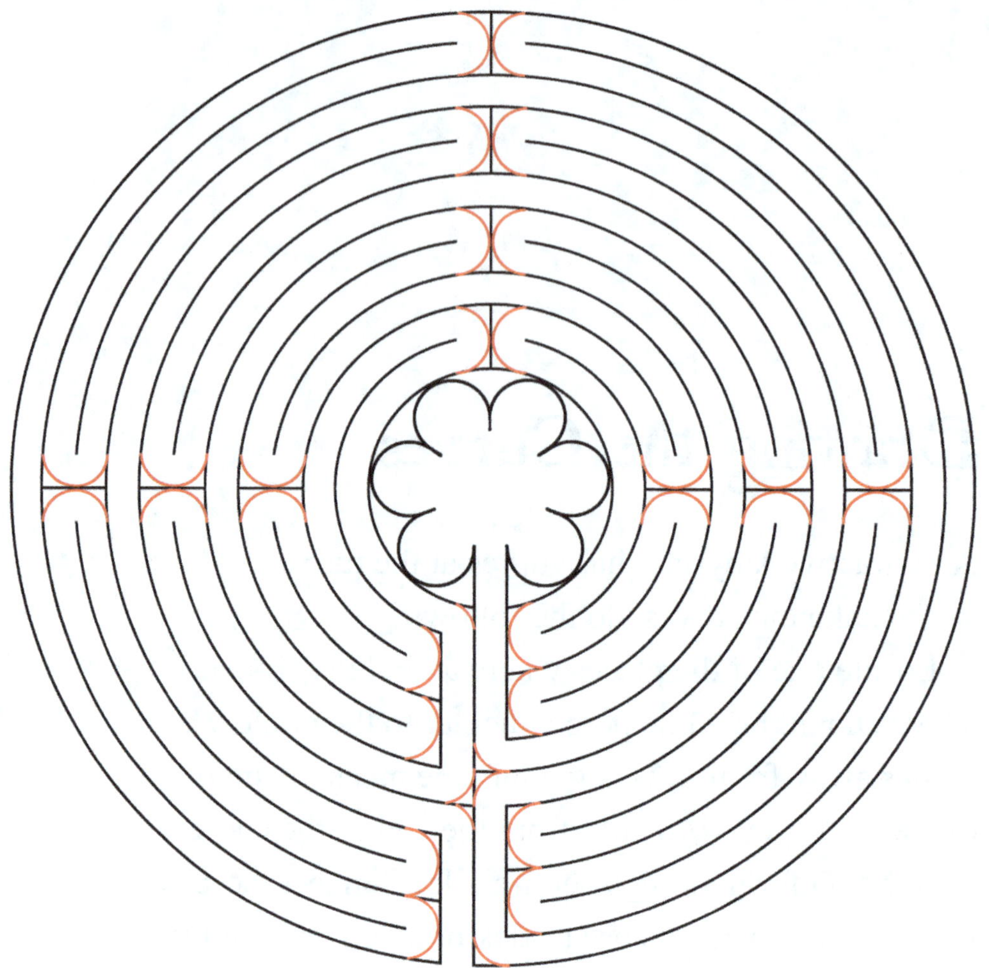

Diagram 12. Drawing the curves at the turns.

Gaps and Empty Spaces: To Fill or Not to Fill

There are some finishing touches to the labyrinth you might want to consider.

As you look at what you have constructed, you will notice empty spaces. They occur at the places where the path turns, in the peculiarly-shaped gap between the ingress and egress paths, and in the spaces between the center petals and the innermost circle.

You can leave these spaces empty, or you can fill them in with rocks.

We debated this issue for some time. On the one hand, leaving the spaces empty gives the labyrinth a light and inviting look. On the other hand, filling in the spaces gives it a more solid and secure look and feel.

What you do with the spaces is completely up to

you. We have seen labyrinths with spaces left empty, and others with the spaces filled in.

 Kim and Mario Build a Labyrinth and So Can You

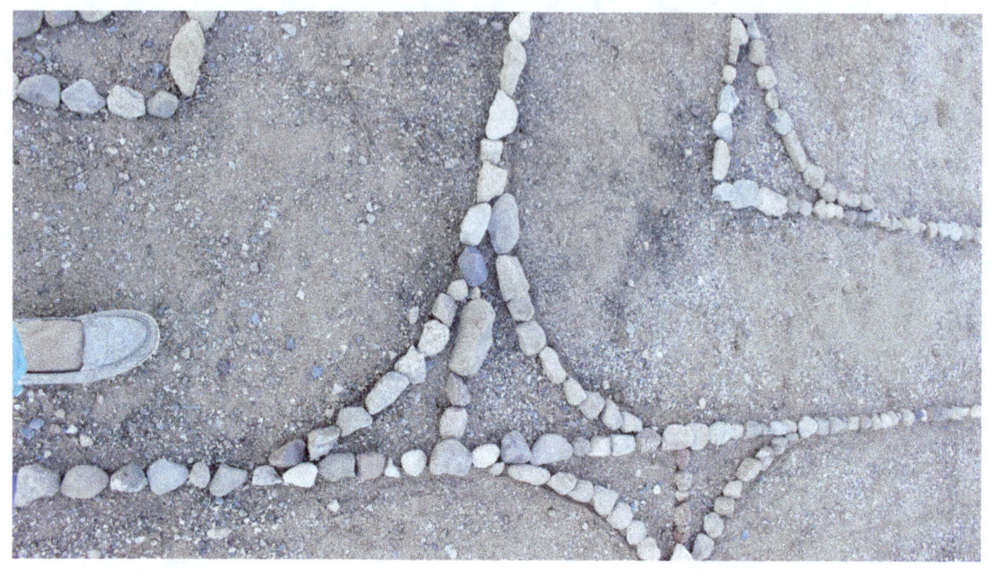

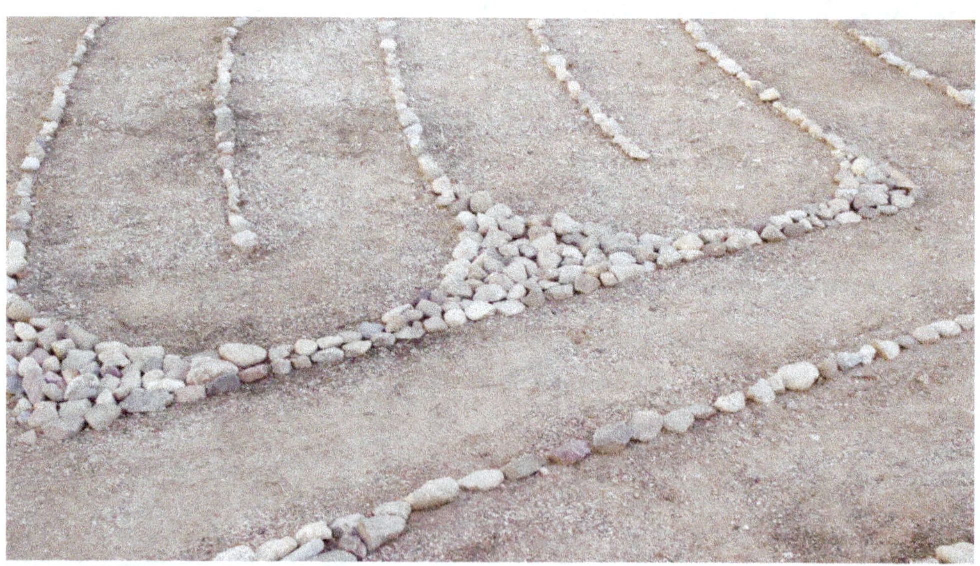

Gaps filled in.

We experimented with filling in some of the spaces.
We liked some configurations and disliked others. In
the end, we chose to leave the spaces around the
petals empty, and we filled in the spaces where the
path turned. It gave our labyrinth a nice balance between solidity and ethereality. We like the result. (See
Diagram 13.)

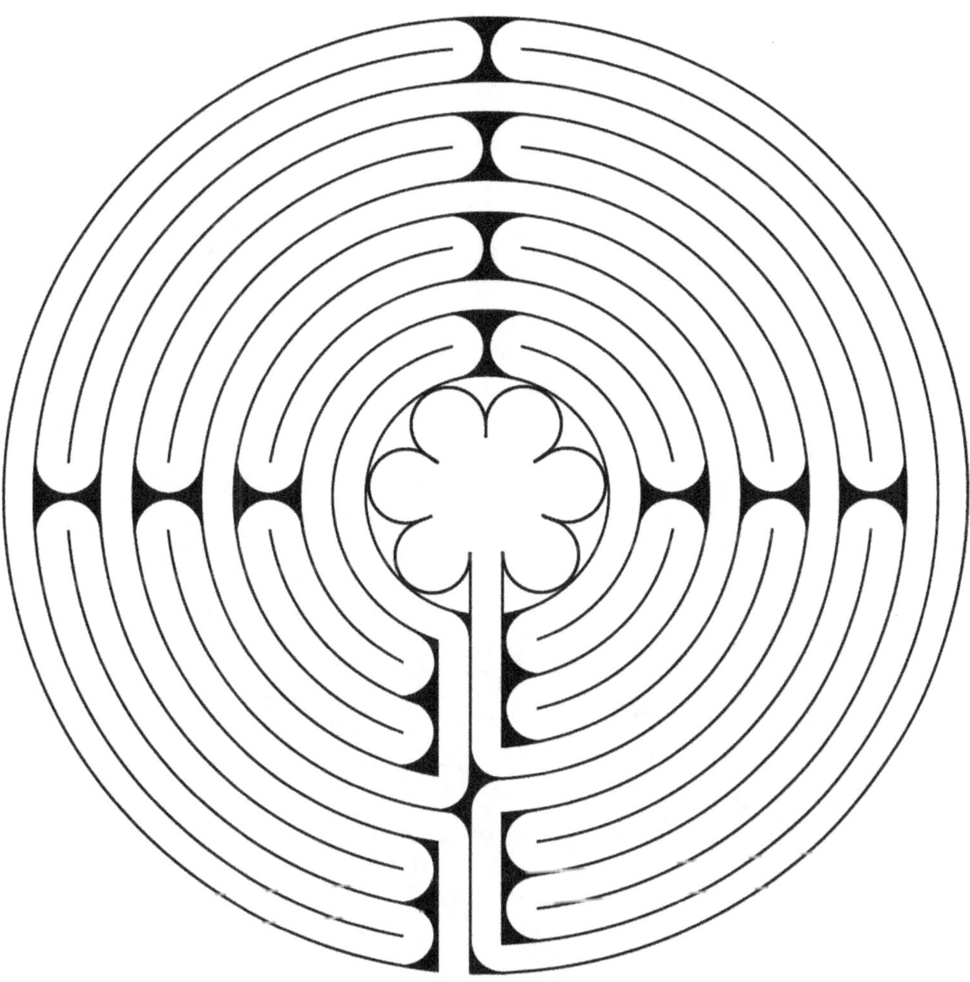

Diagram 13. The gaps filled in.

Fragility and Permanence

You will surely have noticed, as you constructed your labyrinth, that the rocks forming it do not always stay in place. As we worked, we were acutely aware of this. We were mindful that they could be kicked out of

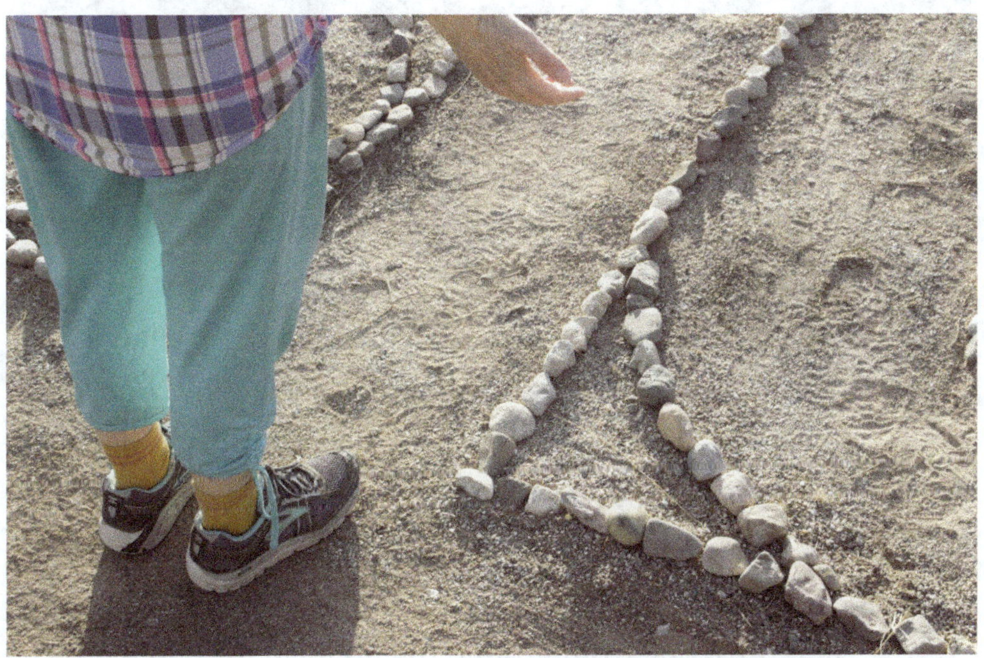

Beginning the walk.

place and took care to avoid doing so as much as we possibly could.

But it was impossible to be perfectly vigilant and

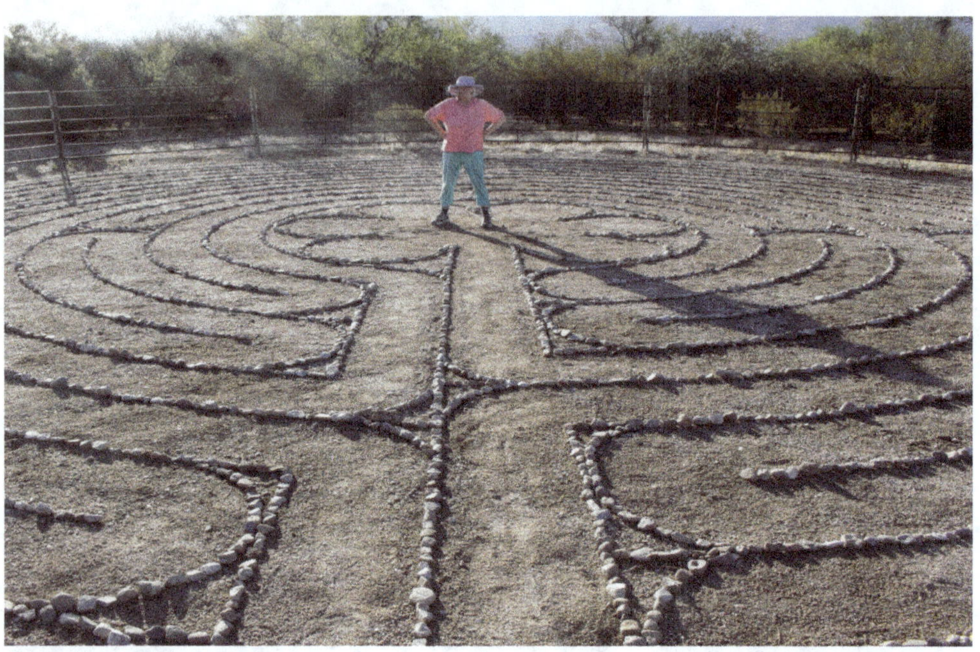

Standing at the center.

we found ourselves picking up errant rocks that had rolled away from their spot in the labyrinth and putting them back in place.

Walking the labyrinth also emphasized for us the impermanence of what we had created. Any labyrinth visitor could kick a rock out of place at any time.

There is a solution for this. Just put it back in its place and continue on.

The impermanence of the rocks also allowed us to ask others to add their rocks to the labyrinth. We invited friends from around the country to send us rocks that we could place in the labyrinth. Many responded, so that in the end we had rocks from Michigan, Maine, New York, New Mexico, Florida, and others.

It's pleasing to walk the labyrinth and see these rocks, knowing that in some small way our friends assisted in the construction of our labyrinth.

And even though our labyrinth is complete, we can still add rocks from other friends or visitors who wish

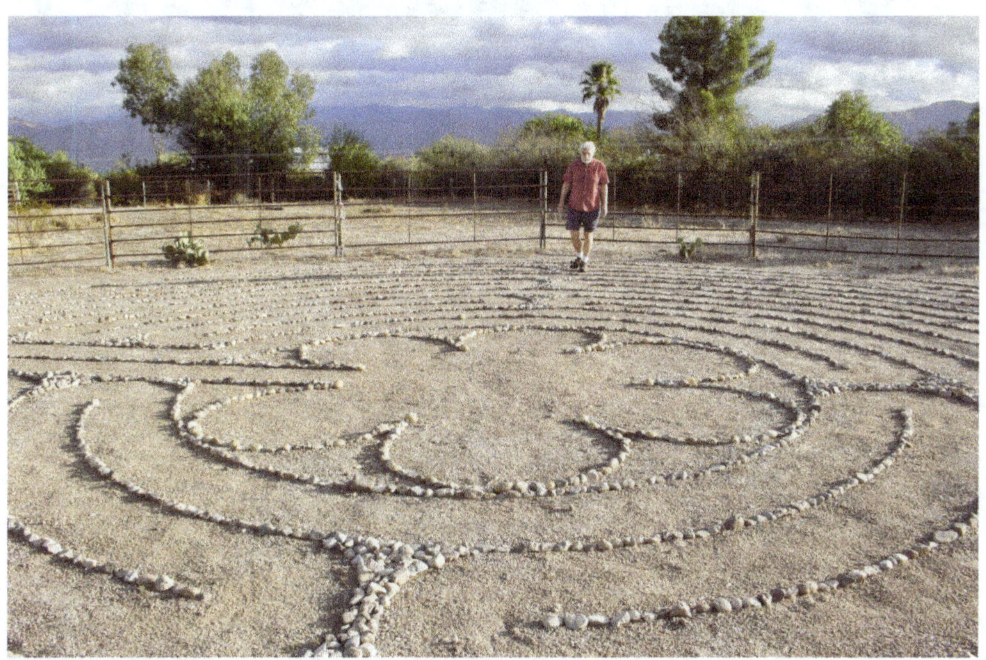

Walking the path.

to contribute. We just substitute their rocks for rocks that are already in the labyrinth.

There are probably ways to make the labyrinth less susceptible to disruption. We could, we suppose, cement them into place. Or nail them down by some

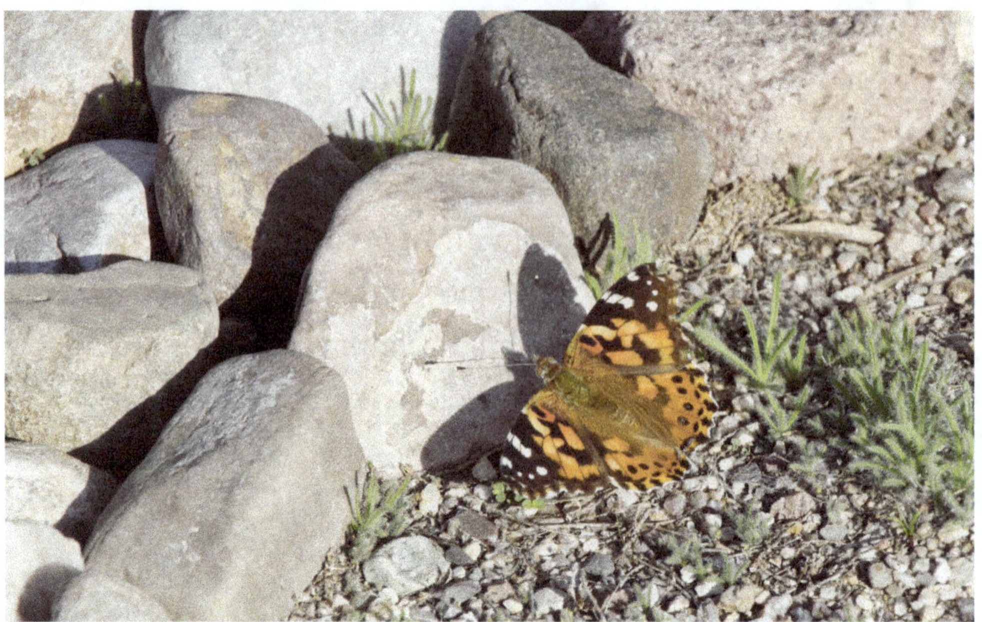

The labyrinth welcomes all visitors.

other method. We chose not to do any of these things, allowing the rocks to remain open to displacement.

It felt like it added a degree of spiritual freedom to the whole enterprise. The rocks were not held to some artificial notion of permanence. They were free to roam and free to return to their home in the pattern of the labyrinth.

But that's us. You might disagree. If you would like your labyrinth to be more permanent, you could place heavier slabs of concrete instead of rocks. Or you could paint your labyrinth on a concrete surface. Or construct your labyrinth out of bricks. There are any number of ways of making a labyrinth.

Some Final Remarks

Constructing this labyrinth was one of the most satisfying tasks we have ever undertaken. It took about six weeks to complete, and each day that we were out drawing circles or placing stones was special in a way none of our other projects have ever been.

A labyrinth is like a formal poem. Just as a poem has a prescribed number of lines and a certain meter for each line, so a labyrinth has a prescribed number of circuits and certain stops and turns in those circuits. But just like a poet, a maker of labyrinths is free to innovate.

Just as no two sonnets are alike, no two labyrinths are alike. You are even free to design your own, with as many or as few circuits as you please, and with as many or as few twists and turns as you like.

We hope we have inspired you to try your hand at making a labyrinth.

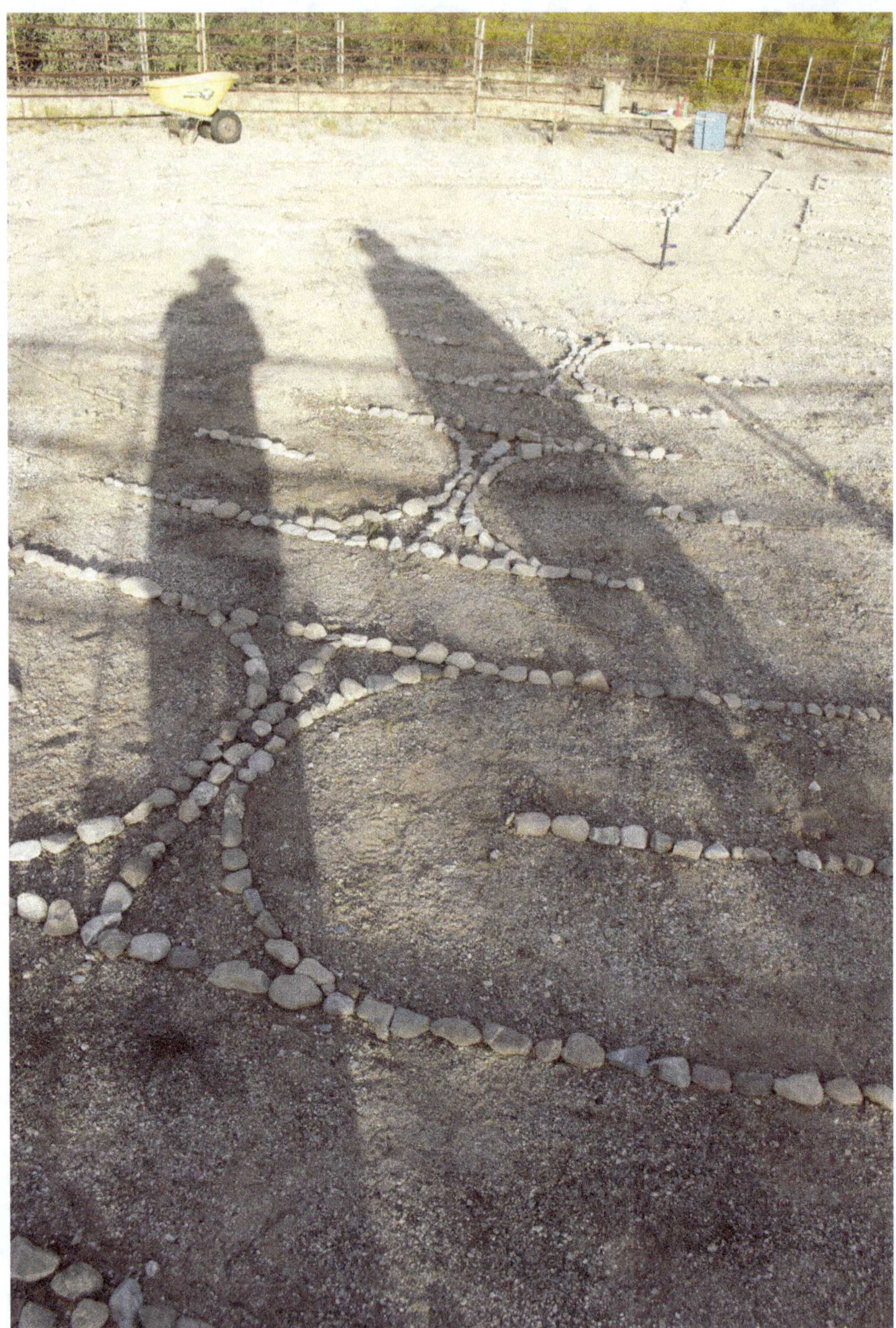

Our shadows falling on our labyrinth in progress.

  Kim and Mario Build a Labyrinth and So Can You

The journey should be at least as satisfying as the result.

Good luck and happy walking.

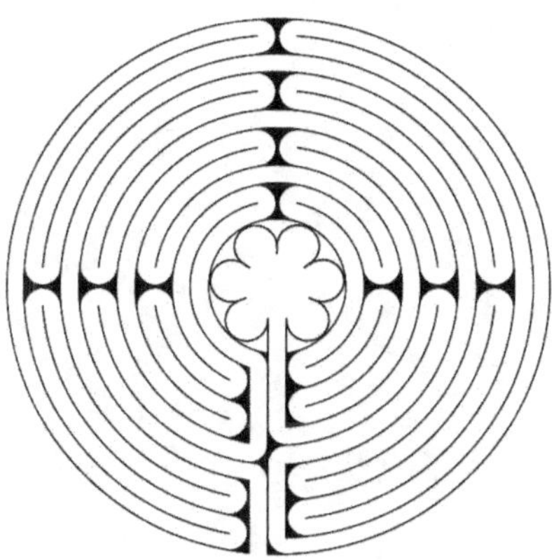

About the Authors

Kim Antieau is a writer and photographer who lives in the desert Southwest of the United States. Her books include *Killing Beauty, Church of the Old Mermaids, Jigsaw Woman*, and many others. She is married to Mario. kimantieau.com.

Mario Milosevic's books include the novels *Labor Days, Splitting, The Last Giant,* and *Terrastina and Mazolli,* the poetry collection *Animal Life,* and the story collection *Mostly Invisible.* He lives in the desert Southwest of the United States. He is married to Kim. mariowrites.com.

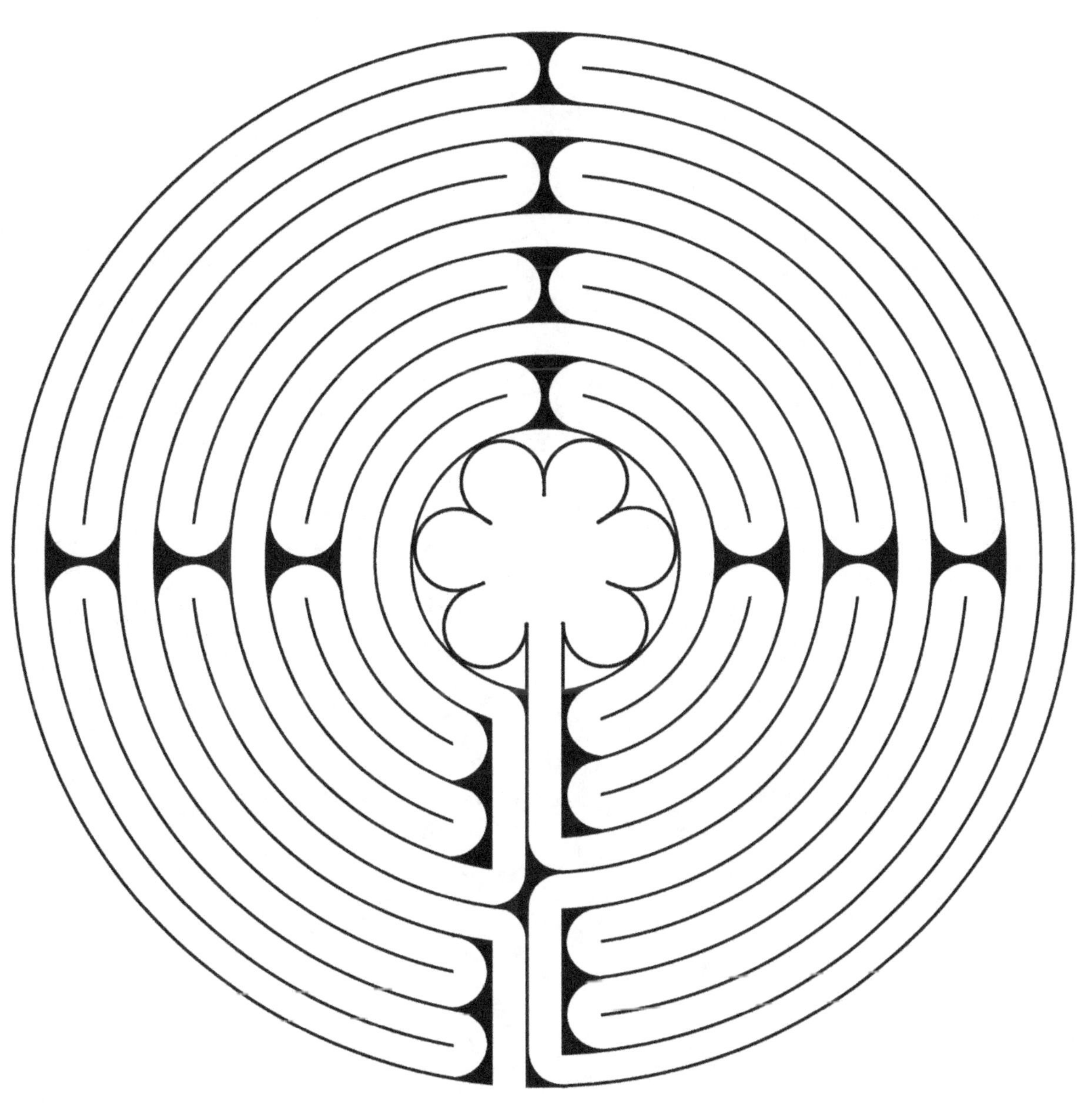